Read the Book!
See the Movie!

Marlon Brando as Napoleon in *Desiree*

Read the Book! See the Movie!

From Novel to Film Via 20th Century-Fox

by Gary A. Smith

BearManor Media
2018

Read the Book! See the Movie!
From Novel to Film Via 20th Century-Fox

© 2018 Gary A. Smith

All rights reserved.

For information, address:

BearManor Media
P. O. Box 71426
Albany, GA 31708

bearmanormedia.com

Typesetting and layout by John Teehan

Cover image: Tyrone Power in *Captain from Castile*

Published in the USA by BearManor Media

ISBN—978-1-62933-382-3

Once again...for Michael

Table of Contents

Foreword ix

Introduction 1

1   *Benjamin Blake* 9

2   *Dragonwyck* 25

3   *Anna and the King of Siam* 37

4   *Forever Amber* 51

5   *The Foxes of Harrow* 69

6   *Captain from Castile* 81

7   *Prince of Foxes* 99

8   *The Black Rose* 113

9   *Lydia Bailey* 129

10   *The Robe* 147

11	*The Egyptian*	181
12	*Desiree*	209
13	*Lord Vanity*	221
14	*The Agony and the Ecstasy*	229
	Afterword	241
	Bibliography	245
	Index	249

Foreword

NOT SO LONG AGO I attended a lecture given by Jonathan Petropoulos, Professor of European History at Claremont McKenna College, entitled "The 'Real' (and Reel) Monuments Men" which was about the Nazi era stolen art and its recovery. He began the lecture by saying that finding fault with an historical Hollywood film is "like shooting fish in a barrel". He then went on to say that although some of the facts may be wrong, Hollywood's versions of history do at least give you some information about something you may otherwise know nothing about at all.

This brought to mind an incident from my childhood. I was attending a Sunday School class and the teacher asked if any of us knew anything about the Old Testament personage Ruth. I raised my hand and proceeded to tell what I knew. When I was finished the teacher said "Well, you must have been reading your Bible." With childish naiveté I blurted out, "Oh no, my mother took me to see the movie." The teacher called my mother the next day and admonished her for sullying my mind with these warped Hollywood versions of the Bible. My mother asked her how many of the other kids in the class knew anything about Ruth. The teacher confessed that no one else offered any knowledge at all. "I rest my case," said my mother and hung up. This sums up how I feel about historical fiction and the movies made from them. I don't recall knowing anything of consequence about Cortez and the conquest of Mexico before I saw *Captain from Castile* at age eleven but it did prompt me to find out more about the subject. Ditto for the movie *Desiree* and Napoleon.

Obviously the content of these movies should be taken with a grain of salt, but nevertheless a great deal of real historical information can be gained from watching them. Before your eyes you can see Ancient Egypt, Napoleonic France, the South before the Civil War, and Jerusalem at the time of Christ come alive again. Relax, give in, and go along for the ride. After all, it's entertainment and not a history lesson.

Darryl F. Zanuck

Introduction

*"Though sober minds may find our play too light,
Your author and your players claim the right—
To serve no moral purpose by our art,
But gaily treat with matters of the heart—"*
— Forever Amber

"READ THE BOOK. SEE THE MOVIE" was once a frequent publicity catch phrase for motion pictures. Hollywood has always had a soft spot for best selling novels. Witness the recent kerfuffle over the erotic novel *Fifty Shades of Grey* by E.L. James. Better yet that the novel is the first in a trilogy. The initial installment sold over 100 million copies and Universal and Focus Features secured the movie rights for $5 million. The subsequent fuss over casting the main characters had readers of the book Twittering and Tweeting their fingers to the bone. A $40 million budget to make the film paid off handsomely with a worldwide gross of $571 million. No wonder Hollywood loves best sellers. And if this doesn't convince you I have only two words to say: Harry Potter.

This is not a new phenomenon. Right from the start Hollywood realized that popular novels made into movies already had a built in audience. By the late Thirties, movies made from best selling novels were nothing new to Hollywood but *Gone With the Wind* proved to be a game changer. Although many films had garnered the attention of readers of the novels they were made from, *Gone With the Wind* set a new standard for public interest.

The novel *Gone With the Wind* by Margaret Mitchell (1900-1949) was published by Macmillan Company on June 30, 1936. The first printing of 10,000 copies sold out immediately as did subsequent printings, making it the top fiction best seller of 1936 and 1937. In 1937 Margaret Mitchell was awarded the Pulitzer Prize for Fiction but she never published another book. In July 1936, producer David O. Selznick bought the movie rights to *Gone With the Wind* for $50,000. The sale was arranged by Annie Laurie Williams, a woman with a reputation in Hollywood as a literary agent who knew instinctively which properties would make good movies. One of her early successes had been the sale of Lloyd C. Douglas' 1929 novel *Magnificent Obsession* to Universal which was made into a film in 1935 and again in 1954.

As soon as the forthcoming film version of *Gone With the WInd* was

Clark Gable and Vivien Leigh in *Gone With the Wind*

announced, the readers of the book offered their very definite opinions on who should be in the cast. They did this via letters to fan magazines and the studio since Twitters and Tweets did not yet exist. Public interest did not abate throughout the filming, in fact it grew to fever pitch. The search for an actress to play the main character Scarlett O'Hara generated more publicity than any prior movie had ever done and the final choice of Vivien Leigh made headlines. When the film was finally released in 1939 it went on to become the most successful and popular entertainment in the history of motion pictures. Gone *With the Wind* became the yardstick by which all other movies adapted from bestsellers would be measured. Film producers, including David O. Selznick himself, would all strive to find another *Gone With the Wind* throughout the Forties and beyond.

20th Century-Fox was well known as the studio where screenwriters were given a fair shake. MGM was famous for its vast roster of stars and glossy musicals, Universal had its monsters, and Warner Bros. made movies with a hard hitting social conscience. But Fox's Darryl F. Zanuck had been a screenwriter himself at Warner Bros. and he knew the importance of a good script. Zanuck's good story sense and ability to constructively edit the screenplays of his writers resulted in some of the best written movies to come out of the Golden Age of Hollywood. Zanuck never underestimated the value of his writers and never failed to praise them when they deserved it. He also knew a good book when he read it. He missed out on *Gone With the Wind* because he had offered $35,000 for the screen rights and David O. Selznick had deeper pockets.

In 1933 Darryl Zanuck left Warner Bros. and, with Joseph Schenck, the former president of United Artists, founded the independent production company Twentieth Century Pictures. During the new company's first year of production, Zanuck made twelve pictures. These twelve included *Clive of India, Les Miserables, Cardinal Richelieu,* and *The House of Rothschild,* all costume pictures with an historic setting. *The House of Rothschild,* in particular, foreshadowed many of the semi-historical films Zanuck would later make at 20th Century-Fox.

In 1935, Zanuck and Schenck bought out the financially floundering Fox Film Corporation and merged it with Twentieth Century Pictures to create 20th Century-Fox. At the newly formed company, Zanuck installed himself as vice president of production. The following year, under Zanuck's new regime, Fox's biggest production was slated to be the historical drama *Lloyds of London*, a largely fictitious story about the founding of the famous British insurance company. Fox contract

Zanuck also had a definite bias regarding the length of movies: "Since the beginning of the motion picture industry, I do not believe that there have been more than twenty-five pictures which have run more than two hours and a half. And these included some of the big epics. I believe, without a question of doubt, that without harming the quality, [a film] can be brought down to a total footage length of not more than two hours and fifteen minutes or two hours and twenty minutes." Zanuck stuck to his guns about this and the running times of some of Fox's biggest films are nearly identical: *Forever Amber* (138 minutes), *Captain from Castile* (140 minutes), *The Robe* (135 minutes), and *The Egyptian* (139 minutes). Even a proven success like *The King and I* suffered from Zanuck's obsession about running times. To conform to his preferred optimum length several musical numbers were eliminated from the film version of the Broadway hit. Particularly in the case of *Forever Amber* I believe that Zanuck's insistence on reducing running times sabotaged what could possibly have been Fox's answer to *Gone With the Wind*, although censorship from outside sources played an even bigger part in damaging the content and the film's chances of greater success. But more on this later.

By the mid-Fifties the popularity of historical fiction had been supplanted by novels dealing with more realistic contemporary subject matter. Fox continued to produce films based on best sellers but now they were the likes of *The View from Pompey's Head* ("Still on the nation's best seller lists one solid year after publication!") and *Left Hand of God* ("From the pages of William E. Barrett's challenging best seller!"). An advertising section in the October 17, 1955 issue of *Daily Variety* declares "We are proud and happy to announce the greatest line-up of best sellers and stage hits in the history of 20th Century-Fox! All in CinemaScope and Color by DeLuxe." Of the twenty six best sellers listed only *Katherine* by Anya Seton and *Lord Vanity* by Samuel Shellabarger fall into the historical fiction category. Neither of them were filmed. In the years that followed, Fox continued to mine the best seller lists for material, producing such controversial films as *Peyton Place* (1957), *Valley of the Dolls* (1967) and, most infamously, Gore Vidal's *Myra Breckenridge* (1970).

In choosing the 20th Century-Fox films included in this book I have picked titles based on novels which were extremely popular at the time they were published. Many of these books are now largely forgotten; a real pity as they are outstanding examples of the historical fiction genre. The same can be said for the movie adaptations. Although they are all beautifully produced in the typical Fox tradition, the majority of these

Susan Hayward in *Valley of the Dolls*

films have been consigned to motion picture oblivion. At this point in time only a few of these movies are still in the public consciousness to any great extent. *The Robe* mainly because of its place in history as the first widescreen movie and *Anna and the King of Siam* because of the popularity of the musical *The King and I*. The others, not so much. After reading this book, I hope my readers are inspired to "read the books and see the movies." There is a treasure trove out there to be discovered in both cases.

Tyrone Power and Gene Tierney in *Son of Fury*

# 1

Benjamin Blake
by Edison Marshall

> *"If I could live my life again I would be guilty of the same crime and be prepared to hang for it."*
> – Benjamin Blake

EDISON MARSHALL (1894-1967) was born in Rensselaer, Indiana and moved with his family to Medford, Oregon in 1907. He attended the University of Oregon from 1913 to 1916. As a freshman there, Marshall sold his short story "When the Fire Dies" to *Argosy* magazine and this was the beginning of his professional writing career. After a stint in the army during World War I, Marshall returned to Medford with Agnes Sharp Flythe, whom he had met and married while stationed at an army camp in Georgia. Marshall wrote his first novel, *The Voice of the Pack* in 1920. He also continued to write short stories and his "The Heart of Little Shikara", which appeared in the January 1921 issue of *Everybody's Magazine*, won him the O. Henry Award that year. During their time in Medford the couple had two children. In 1926 the Marshall family moved to Agnes' hometown of Augusta, Georgia. Their home in Augusta was called "Breetholm" and Marshall would use the name of this beloved house for the Blake estate in his 1941 novel *Benjamin Blake*.

Edison Marshall was a prolific writer of pulp fiction and wrote adventure and fantasy stories for *Blue Book Magazine* and *Famous Fantastic Mysteries,* sometimes using the pseudonym of Hall Hunter. But he also contributed stories to more mainstream publications such as *The Saturday Evening Post, Cosmopolitan, Good Housekeeping,* and *Harper's* the book. Adverse public reaction to Tyrone Power's death in *Blood and Sand* prompted Zanuck to tell his writers to avoid unhappy endings for the time being.

When Philip Dunne turned in his first draft of the screenplay Zanuck felt that Dunne had overemphasized the "social injustice" aspects of the story. He told Dunne "We don't want this to be a social document. It must be told with gusto- swashbuckling." In the finished film, Dunne still manages to give Tyrone Power a nice speech about "social injustice" at the end. While Dunne was revising his script, Zanuck began to feel that *Benjamin Blake* would need another title to better sell it to audiences as the swashbuckling adventure he envisioned. He considered *Son of the Storm* but finally settled on *Son of Fury*. In 1941, anticipating the film version, the novel was reissued as a hardback by Grosset and Dunlap under the title *Son of Fury: Photoplay Title of Benjamin Blake*. Concurrently Dell issued a paperback titled *Benjamin Blake, Son of Fury*.

Before principal photography began, a second unit crew headed by Otto Brewer was sent to Hawaii to film background footage for the scenes set in Tahiti. Zanuck had decided to expand this section of the story. This decision cost $125,000 which brought the estimated budget up to $2 million. Other location photography was done at Pasadena's Busch Gardens. The government rationed the amount of available Technicolor film stock during World War II so *Son of Fury* would be shot in black and white. The Tahitian sequences were tinted in sepia for the initial release but shown only in black and white for subsequent reissues.

Virginia Gilmore was originally cast as "Lady Helena Blake" but it was soon decided that she looked too young for the part. On August 29, 1941, the film was back in Louella Parson's column.

> KAY JOHNSON TO MAKE NEW FILM; LONG TIME AWAY FINALLY PERSUADED TO ACCEPT ROLE IN *SON OF FURY.*
>
> "Kay Johnson is coming back to the screen- and I say that is good news to any movie fan. Kay has accepted the role of Lady Helene [sic] in *Son of Fury*, with Tyrone Power- and, as you know, this is the former *Benjamin Blake* announced for Ty. Bill Perlberg, the producer, tells it was harder to coax Kay back to the screen than it would be to get Helen Hayes. The reason is that John Cromwell, her husband, is the director of the picture and the lady has

a sense of humor for she said: 'What? Make a comeback in my husband's picture and have everybody say it was the only offer I could get!'"

There were other changes in casting prior to the start of production. Edmund Gwenn asked to be released from his commitment so he could appear in the Broadway stage production of the Chekov play *Three Sisters*. Laird Cregar was originally considered for the role of Sir Arthur Blake but George Sanders ended up playing the part. Ida Lupino, who had been cast as Isabel Blake, was taken off the picture and cast in *Moontide* opposite French actor Jean Gabin in his first American movie. Maureen O'Hara was briefly recast as Isabel but had to bow out when she needed an emergency appendectomy. Next up was Cobina Wright Jr. who came down with a severe throat infection. Apparently having exhausted all of the contract players he felt were right for the part of Isabel, Zanuck borrowed Francis Farmer from Paramount. Once filming started, it turned out that Farmer's casting would also be problematic.

In her autobiography, co-star Gene Tierney, who plays the part of Eve, says: "It was during the making of *Son of Fury* that I had my first, up-close exposure to mental illness- someone else's. Francis Farmer fell ill. I heard the crew buzzing and gossiping about her. She had thrown a brush at one of the hairdressers, had a tantrum on the set, and literally snarled at people. I was puzzled by her behavior and by the crew's lack of sympathy for her. Francis never left our picture. By the end of it, no one seemed to realize, or care, that she was seriously ill." *Son of Fury* would be Francis Farmer's last appearance in a major motion picture. When she returned to Paramount she was suspended when she refused a role in *Take a Letter Darling* and soon after her contract was terminated. After several brushes with the law caused by her erratic behavior, Farmer's mother had her committed to a mental institution where she was diagnosed as a "paranoid schizophrenic".

In *Tyrone Power: The Last Idol*, author Fred Lawrence Guiles claims that Power's wife Annabella was anxious throughout the filming of *Son of Fury* because her husband was having affairs with both Gene Tierney and Francis Farmer. This, incidentally, is the only mention of the film by Guiles in a book where salacious gossip always trumps information about the making of a movie. I find this claim to be highly unlikely in both cases as Tierney had only recently happily married Oleg Cassini and Farmer was in not an emotional state to have an affair with anyone. If Power had

Tyrone Power as Benjamin and Francis Farmer as Isabel

as many affairs as Guiles suggests, I doubt he would have had time to make movies.

Typically for a Fox prestige production, Music Director Alfred Newman was assigned to write the background score for *Son of Fury*. One of his melodies would become a popular song called "Blue Tahitian Moon" with lyrics by Mack Gordon.

Son of Fury: The Story of Benjamin Blake (as it was eventually titled) opened in New York on January 29, 1942 at the Roxy Theatre. Bosley Crowther's *New York Times* review begins: "20th Century-Fox and Darryl F. Zanuck have always had a soft spot in their corporate heart (but not their head) for robust romantic screen fiction dressed in historical clothes." He continues, "To say that [*Son of Fury*] is an excessively fanciful film would be a mild statement. For the fact, it's another juvenile charmer with a great deal more brawn than brain." *Variety* felt that the "Running time is a little long, with some sequences slowing the action down, but generally the story commands rapt attention and, on the whole, emerges as sound, compelling entertainment."

Howard Barnes of the *New York Herald* thought Tyrone Power was "at his flamboyant best" and that he "bears the brunt of the acting and bears it handsomely." Author Edison Marshall said that he felt the book and the movie "compliment each other nicely." The film opened in Hollywood at Grauman's Chinese Theatre on February 12, 1942 where, curiously, it played only one week. *Son of Fury* made $1.6 million in the U.S. which made it Fox's eighth biggest moneymaker that year. The film would go on to make a considerable amount of money throughout the rest of the world, making it a box office success.

SON OF FURY: The Story of Benjamin Blake

Released: January 1942. Running time: 98 minutes
Produced by Darryl F. Zanuck
Directed by John Cromwell
Screenplay by Philip Dunne.
Music by Alfred Newman
Cinematography by Arthur C. Miller
Editing by Walter Thompson.
Cast: Tyrone Power, Gene Tierney, George Sanders, Francis Farmer,
    John Carradine, Elsa Lanchester, Harry Davenport, Kay Johnson,
    Roddy McDowall, Dudley Digges

The story opens in the port of Bristol, England. Young Benjamin Blake (Roddy McDowall) lives with his grandfather Amos Kidder (Harry Davenport). Ben is the illegitimate son of Godfrey Blake and Amos' daughter, both now deceased. Godfrey's brother, Sir Arthur Blake (George Sanders) comes to take Ben to the family estate of Breetholm, presumably to give him a better life. Instead he makes Ben a stableboy and treats him cruelly. He is plagued by the fear that Ben is the rightful heir to the Blake title and estate. Ten years pass and Ben (now Tyrone Power) has fallen in love with Sir Arthur's daughter Isabel (Francis Farmer), a situation greatly encouraged by her. When Sir Arthur finds out he beats Ben badly. When Ben fights back his uncle accuses him of assault with intent to kill, which is a hanging offense. Ben runs away from Bristol vowing to return one day and claim the title he believes is rightfully his. He stows away on a ship where he is treated just as cruelly as he was by his uncle. He befriends another sailor, Caleb Green (John Carradine), who wants to abandon ship when they arrive at Tahiti where he hopes to make his fortune pearl diving. Ben decides to go with him. In Tahiti, Ben and Caleb are warmly accepted by the natives. Ben falls in love with a beautiful native girl, whom he names Eve (Gene Tierney).

Ben and Caleb amass a fortune in pearls and when a Dutch ship arrives at the island, Caleb decides to stay but Ben feels he must to return to England to right the wrongs done to him. Back in Bristol, Ben enlists the aid of a cantankerous barrister named Bartholomew Pratt (Dudley Digges) to try and help him clear his name and gain his rightful title.

Ben and Eve

Benjamin Blake's defense on the docket

After more tribulations, Ben gets his title and fortune but realizes that his true happiness lies with Eve in Tahiti.

Son of Fury is a prime example of the type of film 20th Century-Fox did best. It's a well written, fast moving, and totally absorbing story populated with interesting characters. A perfect cast is the film's greatest asset. Power and Tierney, in their first of three movies together, are as beautiful a couple as ever graced the motion picture screen. Their kiss in the final shot of the movie takes your breath away. Francis Farmer may have been undergoing a mental breakdown when she was making the film but you would never know it from what appears onscreen. She looks gorgeous and gives a wonderful performance. But of all the good things in *Son of Fury*, and there are many, the best, for me, is the jewel of a performance given by Elsa Lanchester as "Bristol Isabel." When Ben is trying to escape from England he seeks refuge at The Bull's Head, a wharf side Grog Shop. Lanchester is a barmaid and prostitute named Isabel who works there. She aids Ben and shows a greatness of heart that Ben's other Isabel sorely lacks. When Ben returns from Tahiti he searches for Bristol Isabel and finds her ailing and impoverished. Unfortunately this

Ben meets Bristol Isabel

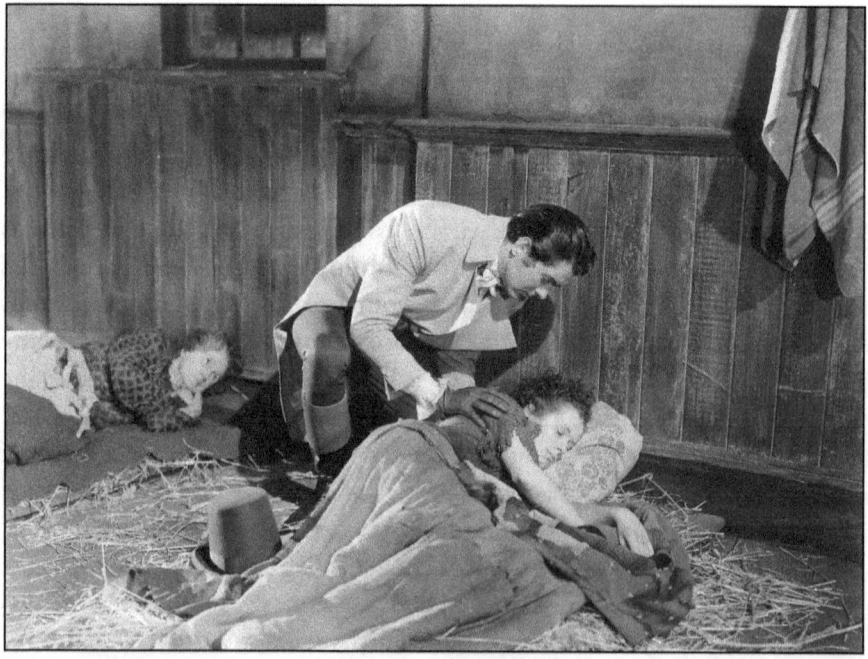
In this cut scene Ben finds a destitute Bristol Isabel on his return to England

latter bit ended up on the cutting room floor. Lanchester's brief scenes are memorable but also a sad reminder of how underused she was by Hollywood.

More than any other major studio, 20th Century-Fox liked to recycle the plots of their films for other movies. And I'm not talking about "remakes". *The Rains of Ranchipur* (1955) was an acknowledged remake of Fox's 1939 hit *The Rains Came*, both based on the novel by Louis Bromfield. I'm referring to when Fox took a basic plot, changed the locale of the story and the names of the characters and hoped that audiences wouldn't notice. *Love Is News*, a 1937 comedy with Tyrone Power and Loretta Young, became the 1943 Betty Grable turn-of-the -century musical *Sweet Rosie O'Grady*. In 1948 they used the same plot again for *That Wonderful Urge*, a comedy starring Tyrone Power (again!) and Gene Tierney. Another example is *House of Strangers*, a 1949 film noir based on the Jerome Weidman 1941 novel *I'll Never Go There Anymore*. A change of time period and locale and it became the 1954 western *Broken Lance*. In 1961 the same story surfaced yet again with a circus setting as *The Big Show*.

Although the credits of *Treasure of the Golden Condor* do say it is "Based on a Novel by Edison Marshall", they don't say which one. Hopefully audiences wouldn't realize this was another version of *Benjamin Blake*. Instead of an 18th century English setting, it is now set in 18th century France. Benjamin has become Jean-Paul, who goes to Guatemala instead of Tahiti. Other than that, the plot is pretty much the same.

In 1946, author/aviator Clayton Knight wrote a book called *Quest of the Golden Condor*. In it a widowed professor takes his two sons to South America on a search for the Golden Condor, a fabled treasure of the Incas. The book is a prime example of "A Boy's Own Adventure" and won first prize in the *New York Herald Tribune's* Spring Book Festival. Publicity at the time stated that the book was based on a trip the author had undertaken with his family. One of Clayton Knight's sons is the famed illustrator of the *Eloise* books, Hilary Knight. In a recent inquiry to him about his father's book Hilary said that he and his brother never went with their father to South America. It was all publicity dreamed up by the publisher. He also said that he has no recollection of Fox ever approaching his father for the screen rights to the book. Yet somehow elements from Clayton Knight's book found their way into Delmer Daves' script for the reboot of *Benjamin Blake*.

First announced as *The Golden Serpent*, the title evolved into *Condor's Nest* and eventually *Treasure of the Golden Condor*. The film was the first

Cornel Wilde as Jean-Paul in *Treasure of the Golden Condor*

Hollywood production to feature location shooting in Guatemala. Like Kay Johnson before her, Fay Wray returned to the screen after a long absence in the same role Johnson played in *Son of Fury*. When filming on *Treasure of the Golden Condor* was finished, director Delmer Daves left for England to direct his next picture. After viewing the completed footage, Darryl Zanuck wanted some additional scenes and retakes and gave this task to Otto Preminger. Preminger later said "It was only one scene, it took an hour" but it is has been conjectured that his contribution was more extensive than he admitted.

Treasure of the Golden Condor was released in February 1953 and went on to make back most if its $1.2 million budget during the U.S. release. Like *Son of Fury,* international engagements put the movie well into the black. The anonymous *New York Times* critic didn't seem to realize that it is a remake of *Son of Fury.* The reviewer says, "Mr. [Delmer] Daves cannot be accused of desecrating his source, a typically sprawling and fanciful novel by Edison Marshall" but the critic doesn't seem aware of what that source is. The review goes on to say: "Filmed in the splashiest kind of Technicolor amid eye-filling backgrounds, this Jules Buck production stacks up as any respectably wrought adventure romp should- pretty and constantly on the go." Not bad compared to Bosley Crowther's condescending review of the original version, which is a much better movie than this one. For once *Variety* was less enthused than the *New York Times* saying "A moderate round of entertainment is offered in this adventure-swashbuckler." Like most Fox films, *Treasure of the Golden Condor* had its Hollywood premiere at Grauman's Chinese Theatre. The film opened there on February 10, 1953 and played a one week engagement.

TREASURE OF THE GOLDEN CONDOR
Released: February 1953. Running time: 93 minutes.
In Technicolor
Produced by Jules Buck
Written and Directed by Delmer Daves
Music by Sol Kaplan.
Cinematography by Edward Cronjager
Edited by Robert Simpson.
Cast: Cornel Wilde, Constance Smith, Anne Bancroft, Finlay Currie,
　　　George Macready, Walter Hampden, Fay Wray, Leo G. Carroll

The film's 93 minute length is divided equally into thirds. The first and last thirds are basically a scene by scene, line by line copy of *Son of Fury*. It's amazing that Philip Dunne didn't demand credit for the pervasive reuse of his dialogue. As previously mentioned, Benjamin has become Jean-Paul (Cornel Wilde). His evil uncle is now Edward, Marquis de St. Malo

(George Mcready) whose daughter is Marie, Comtesse de St. Malo (Anne Bancroft).

The most significant difference in the first third of the movie is the addition of MacDougal (Finlay Currie) who substitutes for the Caleb Green character in the prior film. MacDougal is a Scotsman who has come from Guatemala in search of a former missionary priest who can translate a parchment map he has acquired. When Jean-Paul must flee France, he sails with MacDougal back to Guatemala where the Scotsman's daughter Clara (Constance Smith) joins them on their quest for the Mayan treasure indicated on the map.

The middle section of *Treasure of the Golden Condor* sometimes comes across as a B-movie adventure programmer, complete with fierce natives, earthquakes, and deadly pythons. What sets it above programmer status is the extensive Technicolor location photography, which is often quite spectacular. Unlike other Fox location shoots where doubles stand in for the stars, Cornel Wilde, Finlay Currie, and Constance Smith went to Guatemala for the filming of these scenes.

Jean-Paul and MacDougal find the treasure and the young man returns to France to claim his title and estate. To this end he engages

Cornel Wilde and Anne Bancroft

Cornel Wilde and Finlay Currie

the lawyer Raoul Dondel (Leo G. Carroll) and gives him a retainer of emeralds (rather than pearls as in *Son of Fury*). The rest of the movie plays out exactly like the earlier version. Apparently the artist assigned to design the posters for *Treasure of the Golden Condor* took the title a bit too literally as the artwork prominently features a menacing giant condor. There is no condor in the film at all, giant or otherwise.

Gene Tierney and Vincent Price in *Dragonwyck*

2

Dragonwyck
by Anya Seton

"I will not live by ordinary standards. I will not run with the pack."

– *Nicholas Van Ryn*

DRAGONWYCK WAS THE SECOND novel of author Anya Seton, pen name of Ann Seton Chase (1904-1990). First serialized in *Ladies Home Journal* from August to December 1943, the book came out from Houghton Mifflin Co. in early 1944 and became a national best seller. Seton termed her books "biographical novels" but *Dragonwyck* would be better described as a Gothic Romance. It follows the pattern of *Jane Eyre* and *Rebecca* wherein a naive young woman becomes the second wife to a rather mysterious man who is far above her in social station. The unique element in *Dragonwyck* is its setting in the upper Hudson Valley, New York in 1844. At this time the area was populated by the Dutch aristocracy who ruled it as a feudal state. Patroons owned the land and rented out leases on it to tenant farmers who were forced to pay tribute and were treated as serfs. An Anti-Rent War in 1845 eventually brought about the dissolution of this system and *Dragonwyck* is set during this period of conflict and change. Seton said that her inspiration for writing *Dragonwyck* came from a true incident which was recorded in *The New York Herald Tribune* in 1849.

Only one other of Anya Seton's novels was made into a motion picture. *Foxfire* was filmed by Universal-International in 1955 and starred Jeff Chandler and Jane Russell. The Depression era setting of the book was changed to a time contemporary with when the film was produced.

20th Century-Fox optioned the screen rights to Seton's 1954 novel *Katherine,* which is set in 14th century England and based on the true story of Katherine de Roet who became the mistress of John of Gaunt, Duke of Lancaster. Although a January 9, 1955 press release issued by Fox stated it was scheduled for production that year, the movie was never made.

THE MOVIE

20th Century-Fox bought the film rights to *Dragonwyck* in December 1943, the month the serialization of the novel in *Ladies Home Journal* concluded. It was one of three properties specifically bought for director Ernst Lubitsch. Darryl Zanuck was especially enthused about the prospects of filming *Dragonwyck* which he felt was "a tremendous story of epic proportions" which would be "one of the finest and most powerful films of the year." As it turned out, Lubitsch would not direct *Dragonwyck*. While directing rehearsals for the film *A Royal Scandal* Lubitsch had a heart attack and the direction of that picture was turned over the Otto Preminger. The next project on Lubitsch's slate was *Dragonwyck* and, although he would produce the film, his poor health dictated it would have to be directed by someone else.

Joseph L. Mankiewicz was already a successful producer and screenwriter but he had not yet directed a film. When he was first approached to write and direct *Dragonwyck* he was not enthused about the project and planned to decline the offer. But Mankiewicz greatly admired Ernst Lubitsch and came to realize that it could be a great learning experience for him as a fledgling director. He reasoned, "If Lubitsch is the producer, that's like having the world champion chess player as your teacher for a few months."

Before Mankiewicz could begin work on the screenplay, in April 1944 Lubitsch was sent a memo by Darryl Zanuck saying, "Every woman I have talked to who has read the book regrets that somehow Miranda did not end up with Nicholas." At the end of the novel the main character Nicholas Van Ryn is killed when he attempts to rescue passengers from a steamboat fire. Obviously Zanuck was suggesting that the movie should have a happy ending.

Gene Tierney was chosen to play the heroine of the novel, Miranda Wells. On June 17, 1944, Hedda Hopper announced "Twentieth Century's big plum for 1944 is the role of Nicholas in *Dragonwyck* for which Gregory Peck is slated. Gene Tierney will play opposite Peck." Gregory Peck had agreed to appear in the picture when he thought Lubitsch would be directing it. When it turned out this would not be the case, Peck bowed out. With the departure of Peck, Zanuck decided to rethink the casting of Nicholas. While Gregory Peck would have fulfilled the romantic qualities in Nicholas, Zanuck now began to consider the more sinister aspects of the character. Fox contract player Laird Cregar had recently moved from character parts to leading man in *Hangover Square*. Although the picture had not yet been released, Zanuck was impressed with Cregar's performance and his new image. Cregar had gone on a crash diet and appeared in *Hangover Square* as a slim and handsome version of his former self. Cregar was only 31 years old but had always looked older because of his corpulence. Zanuck felt the "new" Laird Cregar would be perfect for the part of Nicholas, who has an ominous quality that Cregar could convey. Unfortunately the crash diet Cregar undertook for *Hangover Square* caused severe abdominal problems requiring surgery after which he suffered a fatal heart attack on December 9, 1944. *Hangover Square* would be released in February 1945, two months after his death.

While Zanuck was experiencing woes casting the male lead in *Dragonwyck,* Joseph Mankiewicz was busy working on the screenplay. He submitted his first draft and on December 6, 1944. Zanuck sent a memo to Mankiewicz and Lubitsch saying: "The script is way over length, but it is not over length because of too many sequences. Practically all the sequences are essential. What makes for forty pages of over length is that we have over dialogued, in my opinion, almost every episode in the entire picture. They say everything they feel and there does not seem to be anything left for them to dramatically portray." Since dialogue was always Mankiewicz's strong suit I can understand his use of it but I also can see Zanuck's criticism of the same in this type of picture. In a January 2, 1945 memo Zanuck found fault with Mankiewicz's next draft as well. Zanuck felt that "A certain B-picture flavor has crept in" and that the fiery climax in which Nicholas dies was "entirely over-written and over-emphasized."

As Mankiewicz continued to labor over the script, Zanuck finally found his leading man in another contract player, Vincent Price. Price was a perfect choice for the part. He had previously played a similarly sinister husband in the Broadway production of *Angel Street* (aka *Gaslight*). Price had signed a seven year contract with Fox in 1940 which stipulated time off for stage engagements. His first part at the studio was

Joseph Smith in *Brigham Young* (1940) followed by *Hudson's Bay* (1941) in which he played King Charles II. When Broadway called, Price answered and opened in the play *Angel Street* on December 5, 1941. In October 1942 Fox requested that Price return to the studio, which was short on leading men because of the war, and he left *Angel Street* on December 5, 1942. His first role upon his return to Hollywood was in *The Song of Bernadette* and soon he had an impressive list of supporting parts at Fox behind him. Price's first starring role at Fox was in *Shock*. This thriller was

Vincent Price as Nicholas Van Ryn in *Dragonwyck*

filmed in 1945 as a B-picture but was elevated to the status of an A release when preview audience reactions indicated it had great crowd pleasing potential. Price's outstanding performance in *Shock* convinced Darryl Zanuck that he could play the lead in *Dragonwyck,* which was a far more prestigious production. *Shock* producer Aubrey Schenck thought so too. In his opinion "Anything Vincent did was great."

Joseph Mankiewicz submitted his final draft of the script on February 9, 1945. Zanuck approved and it was sent to the Production Code Administration for their approval. The script was returned in March with the following requests made for changes:

> The climax should be changed to avoid any implication that Nicholas committed suicide "in order to escape justice."
>
> Although Nicholas clearly states he is a drug addict they should not show Nicholas "resorting to opium as an escape."
>
> "Because of the prevalence of Oleander in this country, and as a detail of crime which could be easily imitated, we must ask that this dialogue referring to being poisoned by Oleander be rewritten in such a way as to confuse the method."

The ending of the script was changed and the climactic fire, which Zanuck had originally disapproved of anyway, was eliminated. Nicholas remains a drug addict but all references to opium were removed. The request regarding the murder by Oleander was mostly ignored. The changes made satisfied the PCA and their approval was given. Filming commenced on February 12, 1945.

The part of Dr. Jeff Turner, the second male lead, also required recasting. John Hodiak had been the original choice to play the part but, when he became unavailable, William Eythe was given the role. On March 7, 1945 Hedda Hopper said, "When [Eythe] stood up beside Vincent Price, Vincent dwarfed him, so the part was given to Glenn Langan." Fox contract player Jane Ball had lobbied to play the lame Irish maid Peggy O'Malley but the part went to Jessica Tandy. During the filming of *Dragonwyck* Joseph Mankiewicz became close friends with Jessica Tandy and her husband Hume Cronyn. He and his third wife Rosemary spent their 1962 honeymoon on the Cronyn's island in the Bahamas and Jessica would be godmother to their daughter Alex.

Vincent Price approached the role of Nicholas Van Ryn by reading the book several times, but somehow he still couldn't grasp the essence of the character. Finally he read in the preface of the novel that Anya Seton had drawn the character of Nicholas from a poem by Edgar Allan Poe called "Alone". Price read the poem and it helped him to understand the character. In the novel *Dragonwyck,* Nicholas meets Edgar Allan Poe and it is Poe who introduces Nicholas to drugs.

This Poe connection foreshadows Price's later career where he gained his greatest fame interpreting the troubled characters of Poe in a series of films directed by Roger Corman.

In her February 25, 1945 column Hedda Hopper had stated that "Price has one of the most complex and difficult personalities to interpret that he has yet attempted in his career on stage and screen." Price later said that Mankiewicz didn't offer a lot of guidance on how to play the part. This resulted in what Price remembered as "the most curious piece of direction I ever received. He kept reminding me how to carry myself as

Henry Morgan and Vincent Price in *Dragonwyck*

a nobleman. 'Erect, always erect', he repeated endlessly." Price's first scene was to walk down a staircase. When the shot was completed Mankiewicz said "All right then, Vincent. Nice erection!"

As filming continued, Mankiewicz found that Lubitsch's illness had made him "stubborn and touchy." Mankiewicz said "We differed about some of the direction, mostly about where I put the camera." In her autobiography, Gene Tierney said of the filming, "Lubitsch was later seized with the insecurity most of us feel when faced with the prospect that one's replacement might actually succeed. Watching on the set one day, he turned to me and said, 'What have I done? How could I give our picture to this novice? He knows nothing.' I told Lubitsch I thought the picture was in good hands." By the time principal photography finished on May 4, 1945, Lubitsch and Mankiewicz were no longer on speaking terms. When Darryl Zanuck decided to edit out one of Lubitsch's favorite scenes, he wrote a letter to the studio asking that his name be removed from the credits as producer. Zanuck complied and the movie carries no producer credit. Lubitsch recovered his health long enough to direct *Cluny Brown* the following year. This was the third of the three properties Fox had purchased for him. He died of a heart attack on November 30, 1947, eight days into the filming of *That Lady in Ermine*. Otto Preminger completed the film but Lubitsch was given sole credit as the director.

Alfred Newman scored *Dragonwyck* in August 1945 and that same month Hedda Hopper gushed, "When *Dragonwyck* was studio previewed by 20th Century-Fox bigwigs, Darryl Zanuck was so pleased with Joe Mankiewicz's direction, he named him for both *Berkeley Square* and *Lonely Journey*." *Lonely Journey* was an unpublished story by Marvin Borowsky which Fox had bought for $11,000 in December 1944 . Retitled *Somewhere in the Night,* this was the film Joseph Mankiewicz directed immediately after *Dragonwyck*. It stars John Hodiak and Nancy Guild. *Berkeley Square* was to be a remake of a 1933 movie of the same name which starred Leslie Howard. It would eventually be filmed in 1951 as *I'll Never Forget You,* starring Tyrone Power and directed by Roy (Ward) Baker.

Dragonwyck premiered at The Roxy Theatre in New York on April 10, 1946. Bosley Crowther was predictably unimpressed: "There is so much talk in the script and so little motion in the action that the tale rather tediously unfolds. Mr. Mankiewicz and his associates have done the whole thing so ponderously that they have drained it of electric essence, and even of the element of surprise." Fortunately Boz did manage to find praise for Vincent Price: "His moments of suave diabolism are about the best in the film." *Look Magazine* also praised Price, calling him "One of Hollywood's soundest actors." *Variety* singled out the leading lady saying, "Gene Tierney plays the governess and it is one of her most sympathetic roles. Tierney is photographed attractively, and paced well too in the direction, as are all the others."

Dragonwyck opened at Grauman's Chinese Theatre in Hollywood on April 19, 1946 where it ran for three weeks and made $43,700. Although many critics were lukewarm about the film, audience response was excellent. The final cost of making *Dragonwyck* had been $1.9 million and it took in $3 million at the U.S. box office alone.

Vincent Price had now starred in a high profile and profitable movie for Fox but for some reason he was immediately thrust back into supporting parts by the studio. Apparently Zanuck had no faith in him as a leading man. It would not be until the Fifties that Price would come into his own as the star of innumerable horror movies and, as such, secure his place motion picture history.

The next film for both Gene Tierney and Vincent Price was *Leave Her to Heaven,* based on a best selling 1944 novel by Ben Ames Williams. Although produced after *Dragonwyck* it would be released before it in December 1945. *Leave Her to Heaven* would go on to become Fox's biggest money maker up to that time and earn Gene Tierney an Academy Award nomination for Best Actress (she lost to Joan Crawford in *Mildred Pierce*). Price and Tierney appeared in four pictures together. When interviewer Tom Weaver asked Price if he enjoyed working with her, his response was, "She was divine…she was wonderful to work with."

DRAGONWYCK

Released: April 1946. Running time: 103 minutes
Produced by Ernst Lubitsch (uncredited)
Directed and Written by Joseph L. Mankiewicz
Music by Alfred Newman
Cinematography by Arthur C. Miller
Edited by Dorothy Spencer
Cast: Gene Tierney, Vincent Price, Walter Huston, Glenn Langan, Anne Revere, Harry Morgan, Spring Byington, Connie Marshall, Jessica Tandy, Vivienne Osborne

Dr. Turner attends the ailing Johanna

Nicholas tells Ephraim that he intends to marry Miranda as she and Abigail look on

In May 1844, pious Connecticut farmer Ephraim Wells (John Huston) and his wife Abigail (Anne Revere) receive a letter from her distant relative Nicholas Van Ryn (Vincent Price), a wealthy landowner in upstate New York. Nicholas requests that Ephraim and Abigail send one of their daughters to become a governess to his daughter Katrine (Connie Marshall). The Wells' daughter Miranda (Gene Tierney) wants to go and they reluctantly agree. Miranda meets Nicholas in New York City and he takes her to his palatial mansion, Dragonwyck located in the Hudson Valley. At Dragonwyck, Miranda discovers that Katrine is an unhappy child and that there is no love lost between Nicholas and his self-indulgent wife Johanna (Vivienne Osborne). Nicholas is a Patroon who demands fealty and tributes from his tenant farmers who have grown to hate him. The only reasonable person Miranda meets is the local doctor, Jeff Turner (Glenn Langan), who supports the tenant farmers in their Anti-Rent Movement, much to the displeasure of Nicholas.

Johanna dies suddenly and Miranda returns to her parents farm. Nicholas follows Miranda, confesses his love, and asks her to marry him. She agrees and returns to Dragonwyck where it turns out her newly privileged life is not what she dreamed it would be. The other aristocratic families reject Miranda because of her low birth and when the son born

Nicholas rejects Miranda

to her and Nicholas dies in infancy, her husband turns against her as well. Nicholas descends into drug addiction and madness and Miranda discovers that he murdered his first wife and now intends to kill her too. Miranda is spared her dire fate when Nicholas is killed in a confrontation with his tenant farmers.

Looking back on *Dragonwyck*, the two stars had very different opinions. Gene Tierney thought it was "a forgettable picture" memorable to her only because she met future president John F. Kennedy when he visited the set and they began a love affair. Vincent Price said, "It was my first Gothic film. *Dragonwyck* came from a very good Gothic novel, but it was hampered, unfortunately, by censorship, because at that time the villain had to be apprehended by the law. It ruined the end of the picture…However, I think it was one of the best pictures I ever made." In an interview with Tom Weaver, Price says that if only one of his films existed a thousand years from now he wanted it to be *Dragonwyck*.

Irene Dunne and Dorothy Chung in *Anna and the King of Siam*

3

Anna and the King of Siam
by Margaret Landon

> *"There is a man born for every task...and I was born for this one."*
> –King Mongkut

MARGARET LANDON (1903-1993) and her husband Kenneth were Presbyterian missionaries from Illinois who went to Thailand (then known as Siam) in 1927 and ran a mission school there for ten years. Both became fascinated with the history of the country, Kenneth with the politics and Margaret with Anna Leonowens, the English governess who had served the Royal Court of Siam as teacher and advisor from 1862 until 1867. When they returned to the United States in 1937, Margaret began to research the story of Anna who herself had written two memoirs based on her experiences in Siam (*The English Governess at the Siamese Court* and *Romance of the Harem*). Using material from these two memoirs and her extensive research, Margaret Landon wrote *Anna and the King of Siam*, a biographical novel about the time Anna Leonowens spent in Siam. It was published by the John Day Company in 1944 and went on to sell over a million copies.

THE MOVIE

Darryl Zanuck purchased the rights to film *Anna and the King of Siam* prior to the publication of the book. He assigned the project to producer

Louis D. Lighton and commissioned screenwriters Talbot Jennings and Sally Benson to adapt the novel into a screenplay. Their first shooting script was completed and dated July 12, 1945 but Zanuck felt there was too much emphasis on Anna and not enough on the King. For some reason Zanuck regarded the subject as a "genuine comedy" saying it was "basically one of the funniest stories I have ever read." Did he actually ever read the book? There is often an amusing battle of wills between two strong minded individuals but it is certainly no laugh fest. Although the resulting film would have elements of humor, it is far more dark and serious in tone than what Zanuck had originally envisioned.

Elia Kazan was the first choice to direct but Zanuck had John Stahl waiting in the wings should Kazan prove difficult. Kazan had recently directed his first feature film, *A Tree Grows in Brooklyn* with Louis Lighton producing. Although Kazan admired Lighton he was often suspicious of what he felt was Zanuck's preference for commercialism over artistic quality. Anticipating a confrontation over the approach Kazan would take on *Anna and the King of Siam*, Zanuck was also hoping that the ailing Ernest Lubitsch would offer to direct if his health improved. Eventually Zanuck decided that John Stahl was the right man for the job.

Zanuck originally wanted William Powell to play the King with David O. Selznick contract star Dorothy McGuire as Anna. The excessive demands and meddling of Selznick took Dorothy out of the running and Zanuck dropped the idea of William Powell as well. Myrna Loy, Olivia de Havilland, and Jean Arthur were all anxious to play Anna and Zanuck had a definite preference for the latter. He felt that with Jean Arthur attached to the project "the enormous cost of the production would be completely safeguarded." Irene Dunne also wanted the part but Zanuck thought she was too old. When Jean Arthur proved unavailable, Zanuck changed his mind and Irene Dunne was cast as Anna. Dunne's contract called for director approval and she chose John Cromwell over John Stahl. She had already experienced Stahl's reputation as a "screamer" on set when he directed her in *Magnificent Obsession* (1935) and *When Tomorrow Comes* (1939) and she didn't want to subject herself to that again.

During the same May 1945 trip to London where Zanuck would discover Peggy Cummins, he also signed British actor Rex Harrison to a Fox contract. He gave Harrison a copy of the script for *Anna and the King of Siam* and stipulated that he would play the King when he arrived in Hollywood. Despite this, when Zanuck returned to Hollywood Charles Boyer was signed on for the role until a prior commitment

Rex Harrison as King Mongkut

forced him to drop out of the project. By the time Rex Harrison arrived at the studio Zanuck was seriously considering him for the male lead in *Forever Amber*. Harrison told him he was committed to playing the King in *Anna and the King of Siam*, having already done considerable preparation for the role.

Rex Harrison discusses the making of the film at some length in his autobiography and it does not sound like a happy experience. When he arrived at Fox expecting to begin work on the picture, the sets were only just being constructed. Harrison learned that the start of filming had been delayed for two months because Irene Dunne's husband had a heart attack and she was too distraught to work. Zanuck seemed to have lost interest in him and his "lackadaisical attitude" was not what Harrison had expected. He found director John Cromwell to be "rather aloof" and he avoided any discussions with Harrison about the character he would be playing. Although he had initially been enthused, Harrison now began to feel he was "too young and too tall" to play the part and he certainly wasn't getting any help from Cromwell to allay his fears. Filming finally began on November 17, 1945 and shortly thereafter Harrison and Cromwell had a disagreement about the accent Harrison was using. After Zanuck took the actor's side over Cromwell's, the director never spoke to Harrison again. One saving grace for Rex Harrison was Irene Dunne, whom he thought was an "excellent actress". Producer Louis Lighton also proved to be of great assistance, giving far more insight and help to Harrison regarding his performance than he ever got from John Cromwell.

Although it had originally been announced that *Anna and the King of Siam* was going to be shot in Technicolor, a Painters and Carpenters Union strike forced Art Directors Lyle Wheeler and William Darling to have the sets built of plaster, which photographed better in black and white. Building the sets in plaster was a much more costly process than building them out of wood. The sixty seven exterior sets and thirty four interiors were constructed at a cost of $300,000. This was the first film for Lyle Wheeler at Fox and he would eventually become the head of the Art Department. He later said, "Of all the Fox films I worked on, *Anna and the King of Siam* gave me the most pleasure and lasting pride." The principal photography ended in early February 1946, followed by retakes in March. The final cost of the production came in at $2.2 million.

Anna and the King of Siam had it's premiere at the Radio City Music Hall in New York City on June 20, 1946. This is unusual because the majority of Fox's big releases tended to open at the Roxy. Bosley Crowther at the *New York Times* gave it a mixed review. He said, "It is really in the performance of Rex Harrison as the king and in the cunning conception of his character that the charm of the picture lies. A more familiar star might well have botched it good." But he found many of the other performances to be "elaborate and conventional Hollywood" and that "John Cromwell is responsible for much of the over-doing here." In the end he does concede that the film is "worthwhile." *Variety* was far more effusive calling it "intelligently handled and spellbinding despite its long footage." The *Variety* review also says that Irene Dunne "does a supurb

Fox Art Director Lyle Wheeler

job" and that "Rex Harrison shines." In fact, most of the reviews singled out Harrison's fine performance. Alton Cook, film critic for the *New York Telegram and Sun* called his performance "remarkable". *Herald Tribune* critic Howard Barnes said Harrison was "nothing short of perfect."

Anna and the King of Siam opened on July 18, 1946 at Grauman's Chinese Theatre in Hollywood where it ran four weeks, doing excellent business. A Summer 1946 trade magazine ad touted booming box office for the film: "7th week at Radio City Music Hall! New all-time, non-holiday record 3 theaters Los Angeles! First 34 dates outgross *Leave Her to Heaven!*". The movie went on to be a winner at the box office and took in $3.5 million dollars. It was nominated for five Academy Awards including Gale Sondergaard for Best Supporting Actress, Best Screenplay, and Best Scoring of a Dramatic Picture. It won for Best Black and White Cinematography and Best Black and White Art Direction. In March 1947 the film was allowed to be shown in Bangkok without cuts although Siamese historians claimed that 75% of the story was incorrect. Margaret Landon had previously admitted that 25% of her book was fictionalized but that 75% was true. A greater backlash against the story would come later.

ANNA AND THE KING OF SIAM
Released: June 1946. Running time: 128 minutes.
Produced by Louis D. Lighton
Directed by John Cromwell
Screenplay by Talbot Jennings and Sally Benson
Music by Bernard Herrmann
Cinematography by Arthur C. Miller
Edited by Harmon Jones.
Cast: Irene Dunne, Rex Harrison, Linda Darnell, Lee J. Cobb, Gale Sondergaard, Dennis Hoey, Mikhail Rasumny, Richard Lyon, Tito Renaldo

In 1862 Anna Owens (Irene Dunne), a widowed English woman, goes with her son Louis (Richard Lyon) to Siam to be governess to the children of the royal court. Conflicts immediately arise when the King (Rex Harrison) refuses to honor his promise of a house for her away from the palace. Anna and her son move into the royal harem but she continues to badger the King about her house until he eventually capitulates. Anna begins to teach the royal children and many of the King's concubines as well and soon mutual affection is felt on both sides. The one exception is the King's favorite, Tuptim (Linda Darnell), who resents Anna.

Although at first Anna's relationship with the King is a contentious one, they both come to admire and respect each other greatly. When Tuptim runs away from the palace she is recaptured and tortured. Anna goes to the King to beg clemency for Tuptim but he becomes angry at her interference and retaliates by burning Tuptim at the stake outside

Alak (Mikhail Rasumny) greets Anna and her son Louis

The King approves of his new concubine Tuptim

Gale Sondergaard as Lady Thiang

of Anna's home. Anna plans to leave Siam, despite pleas for her to stay from many in the King's household, in particular Lady Thiang (Gale Sondergaard), the mother of the Crown Prince. The untimely death of her son Louis in a riding accident makes Anna reconsider. She remains in Siam to advise the King and, following his death, his successor the Crown Prince (Tito Renaldo).

Anna and the King of Siam had been a considerable box office success but the next incarnation of the story would so far eclipse the 1946 movie in popularity that the original would be all but forgotten. I am, of course, referring to *The King and I*. In 1950, Margaret Landon's literary agent sent a copy of the book *Anna and the King of Siam* to the agent of British actress Gertrude Lawrence, who was looking for a new property to star in onstage. After obtaining the stage rights to the novel, Ms. Lawrence approached Cole Porter to adapt it into a musical but he declined. Next she approached Richard Rodgers and Oscar Hammerstein and they agreed although they wanted to base the musical on the film version and not the novel. Rex Harrison was sought to recreate the role of the King onstage but he was unavailable as he was preparing for a stage production of *The Cocktail Party* by T.S. Eliot. Alfred Drake was approached but he felt the salary offered was too small. It was Mary Martin who suggested Yul Brynner to Rodgers and Hammerstein. At the time Brynner was directing TV programs for CBS in New York. Martin had appeared with Brynner in the musical *Lute Song* several years before and was convinced he would be perfect for the part of the King. She was right. The play opened on Broadway at the St. James Theatre on March 29, 1951 and ran for 1,246 performances, making it the fourth longest running Broadway musical up to that time.

20th Century-Fox still owned the screen rights to *Anna and the King of Siam* and *The King and I* had drawn heavily from the 1946 film version, with much of the dialogue lifted from it verbatim. Understandably the studio got first chance to purchase the rights to film the musical, which ended up costing Fox $1 million. In March 1954, producer Charles Bracket met with Rodgers and Hammerstein to discuss the movie adaptation. Originally the three planned to collaborate on the screenplay but the assignment was given over to writer Ernest Lehman. In October 1954, Zanuck sent one of his memos regarding the running time of movies to Charles Brackett, Ernest Lehman, and Rodgers and Hammerstein. Zanuck stated that the Broadway play ran two hours and forty four minutes and if the movie also runs that long "we are in trouble." He goes on to say, "I may be naive, but it has always been my belief that when you go to the theatre to see a celebrated musical, you go there expecting a great deal of music as well as dances, etc. It is my belief, brought on by bitter experience, that too many numbers or too many reprises in a motion picture musical frequently have the effect of spoiling the very things that were so very good on stage." Huh? As a result, several musical numbers were cut so the film version would eventually clock in at a two hour and thirteen minute running time.

The rights to the musical were originally sold to Fox with the provision that Gertrude Lawrence would star. This became a moot point when Ms. Lawrence died of cancer in 1952 about midway through the show's Broadway run. When it came time to cast the film, Yul Brynner was a shoo-in as the show had made him a major star. Although *The King and I* would be the first of Yul Brynner's films to be released, he had filmed Cecil B. DeMille's *The Ten Commandments* before it. Brynner arrived in Egypt for the location shooting on *The Ten Commandments* only 24 hours after his last performance on stage in *The King and I*. The rest of his part as Pharaoh Rameses was filmed in Hollywood during the summer of 1955. When he had finished his work on the DeMille epic, negotiations began for Brynner to star in the film version of *The King and I*.

Yul Brynner resented 20th Century-Fox because they had attempted to prevent his marriage to Virginia Gilmore when she was a contract player there in the Forties. As a result, grudge holding Brynner did not intend to make things easy for the studio. Fox executive Harvey Grant said "He put up every obstacle you can think of. First he wanted script approval. When that was allowed he insisted on cast approval. Every day there'd be something else." Eventually Brynner did sign on for the hefty fee of $300,000 but throughout the filming he had contentious relationships with both producer Charles Brackett and director Walter Lang. Brackett said, "He would try to goad me. Threaten to walk off the set if his ideas weren't instantly adopted." Walter Lang complained, "If

Yul Brynner in *The King and I*

you didn't agree with him you could expect to be called a bloody fool or lots worse. He would claim that he was really the picture's director, that I wasn't needed."

Fox had wanted Maureen O'Hara as Anna but Richard Rodgers did not. At the suggestion of Yul Brynner, Deborah Kerr, a fine actress but a non-singer, was cast as Anna. Her singing voice would be dubbed by Marni Nixon. Deborah Kerr had only praise for Yul Brynner: "His imaginative suggestions and instructions were responsible for turning *The King and I* into a great movie. If not for him it would have wound up being just another pleasant Hollywood musical. I will always be grateful to him for making me look better than I really am."

The part of Tuptim, originated on Broadway by Doretta Morrow, was going to be played by Dorothy Dandridge in the film. Urged on by then lover Otto Preminger, she turned it down because she refused to play a slave or a supporting part. Then Marisa Pavan and France Nuyen were tested but the role eventually went to Rita Moreno, who was already under contract to Fox.

The film version of *The King and I* was an enormous popular and critical success. The movie had its world premiere at Grauman's Chinese Theatre on June 28, 1956 and ran for nine weeks. It opened on June 29, 1956 at the Roxy Theatre in New York and the next day *New York Times* critic Bosley Crother gave it a shockingly good review (his usually weren't). He wrote, "Whatever pictorial magnificence *The King and I* may have had on stage- and, goodness knows, it had plenty- it has twice as much in the film version. And it is got onto the screen with snap and vigor under the direction of Walter Lang. Most of the memorable numbers are here…the few that have been omitted are not missed in the general extravagance of the melody and decor. If you don't go see it, believe us, you'll be missing a grand and moving thing." Wow. The *New York Herald Tribune* review singled out Yul Brynner's performance: "It is Brynner who gives the film its animal spark. This is a rare bit of acting- Brynner is the king, and you don't forget it for a second." Despite all the praise, Brynner always considered the movie to be second-rate.

The budget for the movie was $4.55 million and it went on to make over $21 million at the box office. It was nominated for nine Academy Awards and won five, including a Best Actor Oscar for Yul Brynner. Although I like *The King and I* very much ("Very much, indeed" as Anna says in the movie), I feel it does pale in comparison to the 1946 film. *The King and I* is a far more lightweight entertainment with most of the "bite" and almost all of the darker aspects of the story eliminated. The end result is closer to the "genuine comedy" Darryl Zanuck had first imagined back in 1945. There is also a romantic tension between Anna and the King which was not present in the earlier film version or to any great extent in the original stage play. However, this romantic tension enhances the story and contributes to the terrific on screen chemistry between Yul Brynner and Deborah Kerr.

Although the 1946 film had been tolerated in Thailand, *The King and I* was banned outright in 1957 and remains so to this day. The Thai government feels that the movie demeans their beloved monarch King Mongkut and exaggerates the influence Anna had on him. When I went on a Travel Agent junket to Thailand in the Nineties we were told in no uncertain terms not to ever mention *The King and I* while we were there.

THE KING AND I

Released: June 1956. Running time: 133 minutes.
In CinemaScope 55 and Color by DeLuxe
Produced by Charles Brackett
Directed by Walter Lang
Screenplay by Ernest Lehman
Music Adaptation by Alfred Newman
Cinematography by Leon Shamroy
Edited by Robert L. Simpson
Cast: Yul Brynner, Deborah Kerr, Rita Moreno, Terry Saunders, Carlos Rivas, Martin Benson, Rex Thompson, Patrick Adiarte, Alan Mowbray, Geoffrey Toone

The King and I was not the last time the story of Anna and the King would be used as the basis for popular (or in some cases, unpopular) entertainment. In 1972, 20th Century-Fox produced an ill conceived TV series called *Anna and the King* starring Yul Brynner with Samantha Eggar as Anna. Margaret Landon was so incensed by this "inaccurate and mutilated" version of her story that she sued Fox. She lost the suit but when the judgement was appealed it was settled out of court. The series ran only 13 episodes.

In 1999, Warner Bros. released an animated film loosely adapted from the musical which flopped badly (it cost $25 million to make and took in only $12 million at the box office).

Yul Brynner as the King, Rex Thompson as Louis, and Deborah Kerr as Anna

That same year Fox made a live action, non-musical version of the story called *Anna and the King* starring Jodie Foster as Anna and Chow Yun-Fat as King Mongkut. Although incidents in the script had been altered at the request of the Thai government, they still would not allow the film to be made in Thailand and, like *The King and I*, the movie has been banned from showing there. In his *New York Times* review of *Anna and the King*, critic Stephen Holden noted that "*The King and I* has become so deeply embedded in our culture that its version of the true story supersedes all others." And this accurately sums up why the 1946 movie is now far less well known than the musical remake.

A 2014 biography by Alfred Habegger entitled *Masked: The Life of Anna Leonowens, Schoolmistress at the Court of Siam* claims that most of what we have come to love about the story simply wasn't true. Oh well, the illusion was nice while it lasted.

Linda Darnell in *Forever Amber*

4

Forever Amber
by Kathleen Winsor

"I'll climb so high he'll have to reach up to touch the hem of my skirt!"
— *Amber St. Clare*

OF ALL THE NOVELS discussed herein, *Forever Amber* came the closest to duplicating the popular success of *Gone With the Wind*. Upon publication, the book was an immediate sensation but the controversy it caused surpassed even *Gone With the Wind* in the public consciousness when *Forever Amber* soon came to be regarded as a "dirty book." Sadly, unlike *Gone With the Wind*, nowadays few people seem to remember either the book or the movie.

There are several parallels between *Forever Amber* author Kathleen Winsor (1919-2003) and Margaret Mitchell and the paths their best selling novels took to the screen. Both authors had been newspaper reporters; Mitchell for *The Atlanta Journal* and Winsor for *The Oakland Tribune*. *Gone With the Wind* and *Forever Amber* were first novels for both authors and their books were both published by The Macmillan Company in New York. The main character of both books is a beautiful and headstrong woman who will stop at nothing to get what she wants, particularly when it comes to the man she loves. *Gone With the Wind* takes place during the American Civil War and Reconstruction. *Forever Amber* takes place during the British Civil War and Restoration. The Macmillan Company hired literary agent Annie Laurie Williams to represent both novels when it came to selling the film rights to Hollywood. Public interest in the casting of each movie was enormous, particularly when it came to the actress who would play the lead. The searches for both "Scarlett" and "Amber" generated considerable media attention.

The filming of each movie would be long and troubled and while the film version of *Gone With the Wind* fulfilled audience expectations, *Forever Amber* did not. David O. Selznick, the producer of *Gone With the Wind,* refused to compromise his vision and kowtow to the censors but 20th Century-Fox allowed their film version of *Forever Amber* to be bowdlerized by them.

Kathleen Winsor's interest in the period of the British Restoration began when she was typing her husband's thesis on King Charles II while they were both students at the University of California at Berkeley in 1937. After college she went to work for *The Oakland Tribune* and, in her leisure time, continued to read everything she could find on the Restoration period, filling myriad notebooks with information and sketches gleaned from her research. She began working on her novel in February 1940 and two years later sent a 2,500 page manuscript to The Macmillan Company. Harold Latham, Vice President of Macmillan, was not enthusiastic about the book, feeling the content was too salacious. J. Randall Williams, the Sales Manager of the company, disagreed. He thought the subject had tremendous reader potential so Latham was overruled and Winsor was informed her novel would be published. The massive size of the manuscript was a problem so Macmillan brought Winsor to New York to help with editing it down to a more feasible length . Macmillan's first printings were double columned and it totaled 652 pages. Later editions dispensed with the double columns and were 722 pages long. Macmillan publicity stated, "Once in a while a novel is written so magnificent in its sweep of events, so glamorous and powerful in characterization, so dramatic in plot that it carries all before it. Such is *Forever Amber,* the story of a woman of superb courage and passion." For once this isn't mere hyperbole; the book is a wonderful read.

Forever Amber came out on Kathleen Winsor's 25th birthday, October 16, 1944, and was an instant success. Controversy regarding the novel's content began almost immediately. Three days after the book's release it was banned in Massachusetts as obscene, a decision upheld by Attorney General George Rothwell, who went on to point out the novel's offensive sections with great relish ("70 references to sexual intercourse!"). *Forever Amber* was banned in fourteen other states and it was refused for export to Australia by the Australian Literature Censorship Board (this ban was not lifted until 1958). The reading public couldn't have cared less about the negative publicity. Despite lukewarm critical reviews, *Forever Amber* was on the *New York Times* best seller list for seventy-five weeks and went on to become the best selling U.S. novel of the Forties.

Kathleen Winsor became a celebrity in her own right; her much-married life continually chronicled in the press. She would write seven more novels, none of which came near to achieving the success of *Forever Amber*. At the end, she lived the life of a recluse in her home on the Upper East Side in New York City. When she died in 2003, her obituaries and literary critics gave the belated praise her writing and *Forever Amber* had been denied during her lifetime.

THE MOVIE

In January 1945, 20th Century-Fox paid Kathleen Winsor $125,000 for the rights to film *Forever Amber*. A clause in the contract stated that should sales of the novel exceed over 400,000 copies, an additional $75,000 would be paid (they did, and it was). In a February 25, 1945 article entitled "Heroines Are Hocking Their Halos", Hedda Hopper discussed the increasing role of bad girls in movies, "If *Forever Amber* can be scripted in a way to skirt possible Hays Office objections, this will be a role to end all roles of this type. Practically any star you want to name in Hollywood would give her eyeteeth to get a crack at it." Shortly thereafter, Fox gave screenwriter Jerome Cady the assignment of adapting the novel into a screenplay. Cady had received an Academy Award nomination the previous year for writing Fox's World War II movie *A Wing and a Prayer*. William Perlberg, who had already produced several successful films for Fox, would produce *Forever Amber* under the close supervision of Darryl Zanuck.

Jerome Cady wrote an extensive treatment of the novel in March 1945 and developed this into his first draft of the script which he submitted in May. Zanuck was not happy with the outcome, feeling that Cady had stuck too closely to the novel, including far too many characters and incidents which were deemed unnecessary. Zanuck also felt that parts of the script would never be passed by the Hays Office censorship board. Cady revised his script and resubmitted it to Zanuck in July but this effort was also rejected. Out went Cady, and in came Philip Dunne…reluctantly. Dunne hated the book and thought Cady's script was "perfectly terrible." Dunne would submit five more versions of the script before Zanuck and the Hays

Office, who were watching this project closely, finally approved. While all of this was going on, the choice of director had been narrowed to Edmund Goulding and John M. Stahl. When Stahl's *Leave Her to Heaven*, starring Gene Tierney and Cornel Wilde, became Fox's most successful movie up to that time, he was given *Forever Amber* to direct.

With the script written and a director in place it was time to start casting. Cary Grant, Errol Flynn, and Richard Greene had been at the top of the list for the character of Amber's great love Bruce Carlton but an actor at the very bottom of the original casting choices won the role. Cornel Wilde was a pain-in-the-ass for Darryl Zanuck. Although by 1944 he had not yet appeared in any big hits for Fox, he continually pushed for a pay hike and turned down roles which did not appeal to him. After nearly a year without making a film, Zanuck finally had enough of Cornel and loaned him out to Columbia in 1945 for a three picture deal (a real comedown in Zanuck's opinion). Two of these films were costume programmers (*Bandit of Sherwood Forest* and *A Thousand and One Nights*) but the other, *A Song to Remember,* was a prestige production (by Columbia standards) starring Cornel as Frederic Chopin. Cornel was nominated for a Best Actor Academy Award and he returned to his home studio as a major star with a huge fan base. This, coupled with the success of *Leave Her to Heaven,* got him the lead in *Forever Amber*.

Of course, the most pivotal role in *Forever Amber* was Amber herself. Margaret Lockwood and Vivien Leigh were early choices but both turned it down. Zanuck decided that the search for Amber would equal the one for Scarlett O'Hara and with that in mind, Fox began testing just about every actress in Hollywood. Maureen O'Hara wanted the part but Zanuck didn't feel she was right for the role. She later claimed he was punishing her for speaking disparagingly of him to one of his mistresses. Angela Lansbury was desperate to play it but Zanuck didn't want to borrow her from MGM. Tallulah Bankhead (of all people!) and Susan Hayward also made tests, the latter being under serious consideration for awhile.

While all of this was going on in Hollywood, tests were being made in England as well. Briefly, a newcomer named Annette Simmonds was seriously considered. She didn't get the part but she did end up appearing in a handful of films between 1946 and 1952. Then it was Brenda Stephenson, a short-hand typist who had never made a film. In May 1945 Darryl Zanuck was in England and attended the play *Junior Miss* in the West End. Appearing in it was a 19 year old Welsh actress named Peggy Cummins. Zanuck felt she had great potential and signed her to a contract with the intention of bringing her to Hollywood to appear in a supporting role in *Cluny Brown*. After her arrival in Hollywood, Zanuck decided to test Cummins for Amber. The test was a success and she was awarded the coveted role. According to Fox publicity, 215 women had been tested for the part. On January 12, 1946 the announcement was made to the press that newcomer Peggy Cummins was officially Amber. Filming commenced on March 12 with a large supporting cast including Vincent Price as Harry Almsbury, Peter Whitney as Black Jack, Glenn

Peggy Cummins as Amber

Langan as Rex Morgan, Natalie Draper as the Countess of Castlemaine, Richard Haydn as the Earl of Radclyffe, Jessica Tandy as Nan Britton, Sara Allgood as Mother Red Cap, Mari Aldon as Bess Columbine, and Reginald Gardiner as King Charles II.

On April 29, after 38 days of shooting, the production was suddenly shut down. John Stahl was taken off the picture and Peggy Cummins would be replaced in the title role. Philip Dunne placed the blame on John Stahl whose direction he felt was "hopelessly old-fashioned." Darryl Zanuck said that Cummins had been taken off the picture because he came to realize she was "too young" for the part. Cornel Wilde blamed it on "the dreadful, stupid script" and the inexperience of Cummins. The studio had already spent nearly $2 million on *Forever Amber* and now they had to start over.

After being dismissed from the first version of *Forever Amber*, Fox introduced Peggy Cummins in the supporting role of Ronald Colman's daughter in *The Late George Apley*. Then she was starred to great effect in the Victorian melodrama *Moss Rose*. Director John M. Stahl immediately went to work on *The Foxes of Harrow* and would later direct Linda Darnell and Cornel Wilde in *The Walls of Jericho*.

Darryl Zanuck prevailed upon Otto Preminger to take over as director when *Forever Amber* went back into production. Preminger agreed to direct the film if he could bring in writer Ring Lardner, Jr. to work on revising the script with Philip Dunne which was fine with Zanuck. Preminger wanted to borrow Lana Turner from MGM for the lead but Zanuck wanted Gene Tierney as Amber. When Gene Tierney was offered the part she refused saying she felt "the story was trash." Zanuck considered his other contract players and decided on Linda Darnell.

In 1943 Darnell had incurred the wrath of Darryl F. Zanuck when she married Fox cameraman J. Peverell Marley. She was 19 and Marley was 42. Marley was fired from Fox and Darnell was consigned to a series of thankless roles such as an Indian schoolmarm in *Buffalo Bill*. To further punish her, Zanuck lent her to United Artists in 1944 for the movie *Summer Storm*. In this film she played a part in direct contrast to the "good girl" image fostered by Fox. Her performance was highly acclaimed and, like Cornel Wilde, she came back to her home studio a bigger star than when she had left. Another outstanding "bad girl" role in Otto Preminger's *Fallen Angel* helped to convince Zanuck she was the right actress to play Amber.

In her July 25, 1946 column Hedda Hopper officially announced that Linda Darnell would play Amber when the picture resumed filming.

Philip Dunne and Ring Lardner, Jr. turned in their new script on July 31 and rehearsals began on September 4. Cornel Wilde, Jessica Tandy, Glenn Langan, Natalie Draper, and Richard Haydn had been retained from the first attempt. Added to the cast were Richard Greene (replacing Vincent Price), George Sanders (replacing Reginald Gardiner), John Russell (replacing Peter Whitney), Anne Revere (replacing Sara Allgood), and Margot Graham (replacing Mari Aldon).

Cornel Wilde as Bruce Carlton

Before filming could start on October 24 there was another problem. On October 16 Hedda Hopper reported, "It may take forever to film *Forever Amber*. Today the proposed picture reached another impasse when Cornel Wilde was suspended by the studio. 'Exorbitant increases in compensation' demanded by him and which the studio found impossible to meet were given as the reasons for the suspension. 'We tore up Mr. Wilde's contract a year ago and gave him a contract with substantial increases. This contract has six years to run,' said a studio spokesman." Hedda added," I happen to know that Cornel has been earning around $3,000 a week." Cornel Wilde claimed his reasons were not money motivated and that he simply needed a vacation…plus he didn't like the film or Otto Preminger. Two days later a salary increase (reportedly to $5,000 per week) got him back on the picture and made him the third highest paid star on the Fox lot. Thus filming began on the date intended but went way beyond the original 99 day estimate.

In his autobiography Otto Preminger said it was "the longest shooting schedule I ever had." Principal photography ended on March 11, 1947 but, after viewing the footage, Zanuck decided something more was needed. At his request, Dunne and Lardner wrote several new scenes and these were filmed from April 7 through April 24. Now Zanuck got out his sheers and began cutting *Forever Amber* to his preferred length. The most startling elimination was the part of Margot Grahame in its entirety. She played Bess Columbine who was the mistress of highwayman Black Jack until Amber replaces her. The film was submitted to the Hays Office in May and their response was that "The finished picture is objectionable because it deals excessively in illicit sex and adultery." More cuts were made and the PCA seal of approval was finally given on June 20, 1947.

Forever Amber premiered at the Roxy Theatre in New York City on October 22, 1947. The day after the movie opened in New York the Catholic National Legion of Decency, which had initially tried to prevent the movie from being made at all, went into full gear and put the movie on their "Condemned" list. This meant that any good Catholic who saw the film would be guilty of committing a "mortal sin." Despite this, over the next several weeks *Forever Amber* continued to do phenomenal business throughout the country. Then the CNLD upped the ante by threatening to have Catholics boycott any theatre where it was being shown for up to a year afterward. Bingo! Many theaters stopped showing the film and business fell off drastically. Fox quickly withdrew *Forever

Linda Darnell, John Russell, and Margot Grahame in a cut scene

Amber from release. The CNLD agreed to lift their ban if Fox would kiss their holy asses and make further cuts in the film. Shockingly, Fox president Spyros Skouras agreed to their demands. A spoken prologue about "the wages of sin" was written by Rev. Father Patrick J. Masterson, the head of the CNLD, and added over the opening credits. Worst of all, the CNLD didn't think Amber was sufficiently punished for her sins in the original ending so they had Fox lop it off, creating a very abrupt and unsatisfying finale.

Sadly *Forever Amber* would never be the same and the cut footage would never be restored. The truncated movie went back into theaters and went on to become the fifth highest grossing movie of 1947 after being in release for less than three months. Despite the large box office take, the $6.5 million production cost prevented the movie from making a profit.

FOREVER AMBER

Released: October 1947. Running time: 138 minutes.
In Technicolor
Produced by William Perlberg
Directed by Otto Preminger
Screenplay by Philip Dunne and Ring Lardner, Jr.
Music by David Raksin
Cinematography by Leon Shamroy
Edited by Louis Loeffler.
Cast: Linda Darnell, Cornel Wilde, Richard Greene, George Sanders, Glenn Langan, Richard Haydn, Jessica Tandy, John Russell, Anne Revere, Jane Ball, Robert Coote, Natalie Draper

Left as a foundling at the door of a farmer and his wife during the British Civil War, Amber St. Clare (Linda Darnell) grows up to despise the puritanical ways of her village, Marygreen. When Charles II is restored to the throne a group of Royalist soldiers arrives at Marygreen looking for lodging at the village inn. Amber is immediately attracted to their leader, Bruce Carlton (Cornel Wilde), and begs him to take her with them to London. Carlton refuses but Amber makes her own way there, inveigles herself into Bruce's life, and becomes his lover. When Bruce goes to sea on a privateering venture, Amber finds herself alone and pregnant in London. Swindled out the money Bruce left her, Amber is imprisoned for debt in Newgate prison. There she meets Black Jack (John Russell) the highwayman and, together, they escape from Newgate.

Black Jack takes her to a thieves den in Whitefriars where she gives birth to her baby. Later Black Jack is killed during a failed robbery attempt and Amber must flee the authorities. She seeks protection and finds it with Rex Morgan (Glenn Langan), a Captain in His Majesty's Guards. Bruce returns to London and the jealous Capt. Morgan challenges him to a duel over Amber. Morgan is killed in the duel and Bruce leaves Amber to go back to sea. Now an actress at the Theatre Royal, Amber is noticed by the aged Earl of Radclyffe (Richard Haydn). He proposes marriage and Amber accepts. On their wedding day, Amber abandons her new husband to see Bruce, who has returned and contracted the plague which is sweeping London. She nurses Bruce through his illness but eventually Radclyffe comes to claim her. Bruce departs for America and, not long after, Radclyffe is killed in the Great Fire of London. Amber attracts the attention of King Charles (George Sanders) and she becomes his mistress.

Peggy Cummins as Amber and Jessica Tandy as Nan.

John Russell as Black Jack and Linda Darnell as Amber

When Bruce again comes back to England, this time with a wife, Amber hatches a plan to regain his love which leads to her eventual downfall.

Although current opinion is that *Forever Amber* was both a financial and critical disaster, the latter is not the case. Reviews at the time were mixed but the majority were enthusiastic. Here are some examples of the good and the bad:

> *Film Daily* – "Monumental production brilliantly produced, directed, and acted."

> *Hollywood Reporter* – "A spectacular and colorful screen drama. Linda Darnell in the title role is nothing short of superb."

> *Harrison's Reports* – "A great spectacle, magnificently produced and photographed superbly in subdued Technicolor. The action moves along at a steady pace and at times is highly exciting."

"Your sins have found you out!" Amber encounters a religious fanatic (Walter Findon) in a cut scene

Los Angeles Daily News – "Amorously tame... monumentally dull."

Life Magazine – "Deprived of beds, the famous trull seems merely dull."

Family Circle – "Surprise! Darryl Zanuck has actually done it! *Forever Amber* is a good motion picture by almost any standard."

Some thoughts on *Forever Amber*. Considering that I have previously written an entire book on the subject of *Forever Amber*, I admit that I am a bit obsessed by the subject (probably a great understatement). Although I do love *Forever Amber* as it is, I also consider it to be one of the most glaring examples of missed potential in a movie. The Final Shooting script that I have is 153 pages long. If everything in this script had been included, the movie would probably have run about 30 minutes longer than it does. Most of the scenes which were eliminated (they were all shot and exist in stills) advance the story and in some instances were crucial, particularly when it comes to character development.

One of the most egregious omissions was the first love scene between Amber and Bruce which takes place in the forest near the village inn where they meet. This scene established much of the motivation for both characters and explained Amber's unusual name: "[Amber's] the stuff they use to make jewelry- smooth- and when you hold it to the light- it shines like gold." Also missing are the majority of scenes set in the thieves den in Whitefriars where Black Jack takes Amber after they escape from prison. These scenes would have further emphasized the reasons for Amber's desperation to free herself from the situation in which she is trapped. And how unfortunate to lose the entire performance of Margot Grahame as Bess.

Here is what would have been Margot Grahame's first scene in the movie:

INT. ROOM

A squalid place, its squalor set off by the curious conglomeration of furniture: tarnished gilt mirrors, brocaded chairs and several couches. It is on one of these that Black Jack [John Russell] *puts Amber. She is three-quarters*

Plotting a robbery: Mari Aldon, Sara Allgood, Peggy Cummins and Peter Whitney

Same robbery, different cast: Linda Darnell, Anne Revere, Margot Grahame, and John Russell

unconscious, moaning and turning from side to side [she is in labor]. *The room is dark. Black Jack goes to light a candle standing on a piece of furniture near the couch. As he does so the door bursts open and BESS COLUMBINE* [Margot Grahame] *rushes in. She is a luscious, if slatternly wench. She puts her arms possessively round Black Jack.*

BESS: Jack! I thought ye'd never get out!

BLACK JACK (*grinning*): Easy now, Bess- you'll crack my ribs!

At this point she sees Amber over her shoulder, glaring at her with a sharp intake of breath.

BESS: Who's she?

BLACK JACK: A likely wench I found in Newgate. You'll be teaching her our trade.

BESS: I'll teach her to keep out of places she isn't wanted!

She advances on Amber, but Black Jack catches her.

BLACK JACK: Now then, Bess, let's have no trouble. There's room here for all.

BESS: Not for me and her! Not in the same house!

She grabs Amber by the shoulders and shakes her violently.

BESS: Ah- you milk-faced she-goat!

BLACK JACK (*drags her away*): Let her be!

BESS (*screaming*): I'll slit her throat!

BLACK JACK (*shaking her*): I'm warnin' ye!

Then both turn as a cool imperious voice cuts across the scene.

RED CAP (off screen): What's the meaning of this?

WIDER ANGLE
as Mother Red Cap [Anne Revere] enters. A woman of fifty, severe and collected, she is primly attired in black and white collar and cuffs and a red cap, which gives her her name.

Thanks to the CNLD this is now the final shot in Forever Amber

> BESS: *Mother Red Cap! He's brought his prison doxy home with him. I'll kill the wench.*
>
> RED CAP: *Go to your room.*
>
> *Though she speaks quietly, it is with the manner of one accustomed to obedience. Bess glares and stalks out, slamming the door. Mother Red Cap looks at Black Jack, then at Amber on the couch.*

A pity to lose such a good scene, but, of course, the truncated ending demanded by the CNDL is the greatest offense committed against the film. Amber, forced to leave Whitehall Palace by King Charles (George Sanders), is approached by Sir Thomas Dudley (Robert Coote), the King's Equerry, who suggests they have supper. For Amber, who has been the mistress of the King, this is an insult and she turns him down. Later, now having lost Bruce, the one man she truly loves, and their child, Amber despondently informs her maid Nan (Jessica Tandy) that she will accept Sir Thomas' invitation to supper. The last shot of the film showed Amber mechanically applying her makeup in the mirror as she contemplates how far she has fallen. The cut version demanded by the CNDL ends as Amber watches Bruce and their son walk out of her life. Curiously they failed to see the tragedy of the original last scene and somehow perceived it as a triumph for Amber. In all probability the original ending and all the other scenes which were cut are lost forever. Now that *Forever Amber* has already been widely released on DVD, it is doubtful that Fox will ever make any attempt to find the missing footage and restore it. Why should they? The movie, which was once the talk of America, is now no more than an expensive footnote in the studio's history.

Rex Harrison in *The Foxes of Harrow*

5

The Foxes of Harrow
by Frank Yerby

"You look at me as if you own me...as if I'm your slave."
— Odalie

FRANK YERBY (1916-1991) has the distinction of being the first African-American author to have a best seller and the first to have his book sold to Hollywood. Yerby had no luck writing about "the black experience" during the late Thirties and early Forties. Publishers were not interested in the subject. Yerby came to New York in 1944 and there he met literary agent Helen Strauss. He had just won the O. Henry Memorial Award for a short story he had written for *Harper's Magazine*. Strauss got him a commission at Dial Press to write a novel and this became *The Foxes of Harrow*, which was published in 1946. It was the first of thirty three novels that Yerby would write and the most successful, selling over a million copies in a year.

20th Century-Fox quickly bought the movie rights to *The Foxes of Harrow* for $150,000. Yerby had a clause in the contract stating that none of the "colored characters" would be "debased". In an interview at the time he said, "I painted them as they were- human beings with human qualities- and if it's filmed, they must remain that way." Unfortunately, Yerby was later criticized by the black community because it was felt that the characters in his novels were stereotypes and that he shouldn't be wasting his talent writing romantic fiction. In protest of the racial discrimination in the U.S. Frank Yerby moved to Europe in 1955, first to France and later settling permanently in Madrid, Spain. His last novel, *McKenzie's Hundred*, was published in 1986.

THE MOVIE

Jerome Cady, given another chance after his unsuccessful attempt at *Forever Amber*, wrote the first treatment for *The Foxes of Harrow* in July 1946. Darryl Zanuck told him to concentrate on the story of the "principal characters" in the novel, which actually meant that Cady should leave out the black element almost entirely. Zanuck blamed this decision on the Hays Office Production Code which was particularly strict when it came to elements of miscegenation in movies. Cady produced a sanitized version of the story which was later discarded when Wanda Tuchock wrote her screenplay for the film…not that her script was any less sanitized. In the novel the main character Stephen Fox has a New Orleans mistress named Desiree who is a quadroon, meaning one-quarter black. The Hays Office suggested that her character be completely eliminated. Desiree does appear in the movie although there is no indication of her mixed ethnicity. Another character, Tante Caleen, originally played a large part in the screenplay but the Hays Office insisted that her character "be reduced to a part of less importance in the story." Despite this demand, A.C.H. Billbrew as Tante Caleen has the largest role played by a black actor in *The Foxes of Harrow*.

John Stahl, fresh from his dismissal from *Forever Amber*, was chosen to direct. Obviously Zanuck let bygones be bygones. Casting speculation had begun even before the script had been finished. In May 1946, Hedda Hopper thought that *The Foxes of Harrow* might be the film which would bring the elusive James Mason from England to Hollywood. According to her, Mason had read the book and liked it. Fox, on the other hand, had pegged Gregory Peck for the part of Stephen Fox. Peck preferred to be in *Gentlemen's Agreement*, despite objections from his agent due to the controversial subject matter. Instead Rex Harrison, who had scored a great personal success in *Anna and the King of Siam*, got the lead in *The Foxes of Harrow*. He approached the role with much enthusiasm: "I liked the script, and thought that at last I was getting into my stride, because this was a good part." Unlike his experience with John Cromwell on *Anna and the King of Siam*, Harrison would get a lot of help from director John Stahl and he was grateful for what Stahl taught him about film acting.

Maureen O'Hara, who plays the female lead, Odalie D'Arceneaux, did not get along with her leading man. In her autobiography she says that when the camera was on her face and his back "he'd belch in my face." Perhaps this was in reaction to her annoyingly petulant performance.

John Stahl and
Rex Harrison

Maureen O'Hara and Rex Harrison

Maureen O'Hara played the feisty vixen, at odds with her leading man until the final reel, in more movies than I care to remember. In *The Foxes of Harrow* she is actually more sullen than feisty. O'Hara also said that Darryl Zanuck took her to task for being too long in the ladies room during the filming, saying "Time is money." She told him that she had contracted ring worm on her leg in the "filthy, stinking toilets on the back lot and took so long because she was changing the dressing on her leg." Charming.

Vanessa Brown, who played Maureen O'Hara's sister in the film said, "[Maureen] was so mean to Rex- really mean. She would spread around the set that Rex was a difficult man. She was just a horror on that set, absolutely awful, but I never saw Rex retaliate." O'Hara would also make loud anti-semitic remarks in earshot of Harrison, knowing that his wife, Lilli Palmer, was Jewish. Vanessa Brown said: "It was awful, the anti-semitism that was coming out of her mouth. There was no cause for it. It was just part of her venomous self at that point." The gentlemanly Harrison never said more than it was "an unfortunate experience with Miss O'Hara" although when he was asked to have lunch with her for the sake of publicity, he refused. Sadly, a role that he had initially been enthusiastic about was ruined by his vitriolic leading lady who turned the filming into an unpleasant ordeal.

Dorothy Dandridge was originally cast in the minor role of the maid Zerline but when filming began it was Helen Crozier who played the part. On April 30, Patricia Medina and her husband Richard Greene were visiting the set of *The Foxes of Harrow* and John Stahl offered her the role of Desiree on the spot. In the novel the part of Desiree is much more crucial to the plot than in the movie, but Patricia Medina looks stunning in the part and makes her brief scenes memorable.

On May 13, 1947, Louella Parsons ran a blurb about Billy Ward when he was cast as Etienne, the son of Rex Harrison and Maureen O'Hara in *The Foxes of Harrow*. Billy is quoted as saying, "I think I look more like the son of Linda Darnell and Cornel Wilde", referring to his part in *Forever Amber*. In both films the part of the son at age 3 is played by Jimmy Lagano and then at age 6 is played by Billy Ward. During the filming of *The Foxes of Harrow* an article appeared in *Hollywood Reporter* claiming that after he broke his arm Billy Ward was replaced in the role of Etienne by Jimmy Moss. Possibly it is Jimmy Moss in the death bed scene, where the child is never shown clearly, but it is most certainly Billy Ward the rest of the time. Prior to *Forever Amber*, Billy (also known as William "Perry" Ward) had appeared in *This Love of Ours*, *To Each His Own*, and *Experiment Perilous*

Patricia Medina as Desiree

but he seems to have dropped out of movies altogether after *The Foxes of Harrow*. The last reference I could find on him said he was managing a resort hotel in Florida during the Sixties.

Typically for a prestige Fox production, *The Foxes of Harrow* premiered at the Roxy Theatre in New York City on September 24, 1947. The next day *New York Times* critic Bosley Crowther gave it one of his

Billy Ward and Rex Harrison

worst reviews saying "This orotund picture…manifests over-stuffing with the fattiest romantic cliches. The writing is dull, the dialogue pompous, the settings conspicuously faked and the performances are embarrassingly attitudinized." But did you like it Boz? Given the antebellum South setting, comparisons to *Gone With the Wind* were inevitable. Bosley accused author Yerby and Fox of trading in on this saying "Do you mind if we call its effort The O'Hara of 20th Century-Fox?" Although *Variety* predicted it would not play well in the South, the reviewer had far more positive things to say: "Exciting story has strong production, vivid developments, nice performances. Harrison is perfect as the suave gambler and O'Hara carries the dramatic scenes with surprising skill." The Hollywood premiere on October 10, 1947 was at Grauman's Chinese Theatre where it played for three weeks. *The Foxes of Harrow* ended up costing $2.75 million and went on to make $3.15 million in the U.S. alone. In November 1947 the film was number one at the box office followed by DeMille's *Unconquered* and *Forever Amber*. It was nominated for an Academy Award for Best Black and White Art Direction.

The same month the movie was released, Frank Yerby was commissioned by Fox to write a sequel to *The Foxes of Harrow* but the outline he presented to the studio was rejected. Two more Yerby novels were filmed, both of them swashbucklers made by Columbia Pictures. *The Golden Hawk* was released in 1952 and starred Rhonda Fleming and Sterling Hayden. *The Saracen Blade* was released in 1954 and starred Ricardo Montalban and Betta St. John. They were both produced by B-Movie kingpin Sam Katzman.

THE FOXES OF HARROW

Released: September 1947. Running time: 117 minutes
Produced by William A. Bacher
Directed by John M. Stahl
Screenplay by Wanda Tuchock.
Music by David Buttolph
Cinematography by Joseph LaShelle
Edited by James B. Clark
Cast: Rex Harrison, Maureen O'Hara, Richard Haydn, Vanessa Brown, Victor McLaglen, Patricia Medina, Gene Lockhart, Dennis Hoey, Hugo Haas, Roy Roberts

The story opens in Ireland in the year 1795 when an illegitimate son is born to a daughter of the House of Harrow. The Master of Harrow (Dennis Hoey) gives the child away to be brought up by a farmer and his wife. By 1827 this unwanted child has become a gambler on the Mississippi named Stephen Fox (Rex Harrison). He arrives in New Orleans where he makes the acquaintance of the aristocratic D'Arceneaux family and is immediately drawn to the older daughter Odalie (Maureen O'Hara). Believing him to be a scoundrel and beneath her social station,

Randy Stuart as the mother of Stephen Fox

Odalie and Stephen on their wedding night

Odalie continually rejects his attempts to woo her. Stephen wins a run down plantation in a card game and decides to turn it into a showplace called Harrow where he can live the grand life he was denied in Ireland. Eventually he wins over Odalie but a misunderstanding on their wedding night drives a wedge between them.

After that first night Odalie refuses to allow Stephen into their marriage bed but she discovers she is already pregnant with his child. During this time, Stephen and Odalie live like strangers and Stephen takes a mistress named Desiree (Patricia Medina). Odalie gives birth to a boy and they name him Etienne. Stephen is disturbed to learn that this son has a slightly crippled foot. Determined to overcome Etienne's handicap, Stephen drives the child hard and Odalie disapproves. When Etienne (Billy Ward) is six years old, Odalie tells Stephen she wants to take the boy away and bring him up on her own terms. Etienne overhears the ensuing argument and when Stephen threatens to strike Odalie, he rushes to help his mother but slips and falls down the staircase. Etienne dies of his injuries and Stephen leaves Harrow to live with Desiree in New Orleans. During the Bank Panic of 1837, Stephen loses his entire fortune. It is only through the efforts of Odalie that Harrow is not taken too. She goes to Stephen and begs him to return so she can give him another son. Hoping to start a new life together, they reconcile at Etienne's grave.

As you can probably deduce from this brief synopsis, the black characters are given short shrift in the movie version of *The Foxes of Harrow*. The main exception to this is a subplot involving a newly acquired slave known as La Belle Sauvage (Suzette Harbin). The scenes involving Belle are some of the most powerful in the movie. When she gives birth to a son, she would rather see him die than be brought up as a slave. She runs with her baby to the banks of the Mississippi and tries to throw him in. Before she can, the baby is taken from her by Stephen Fox. Belle hurls herself into the river and drowns. The child is named Little Inch (played by Rene Beard, whose younger brother was "Stymie" in *The Little Rascals*) and he becomes the companion of Etienne.

There were some major changes made to the story in the transition from page to screen. The 1795 prologue in the film is not in the novel. Although it is made quite clear in the book that Stephen Fox is illegitimate, there is very little information given about the circumstances of his birth. The film's prologue is a good addition to the plot. Another major change

Henri D'Arceneaux (Gene Lockhart) with Aurore, Odalie, and Andre LeBlanc

from the book concerns Aurore, the younger sister of Odalie. In the movie, Aurore (Vanessa Brown) happily marries Stephen's best friend Andre LeBlanc (Richard Haydn). In the novel Aurore is also in love with Stephen. Andre loves her but when he realizes that she loves Stephen he marries someone else.

One of the greatest differences between the novel and the film is in the character of Odalie. In the novel Odalie is sexually frigid. On their wedding night she rejects Stephen, although she does love him; "Odalie lay weeping across the great bed. She had intended to submit. She wanted to be a good wife…but this thing- this horror of being touched- this dwelling within the sanctity of her person was too strong. The fear was too strong and she could not let it go." This is the wedge that drives them apart and Odalie anguishes over it. It is easy to sympathize with her character in the novel but in the movie version she just comes across as an unsympathetic bitch.

The film of *The Foxes of Harrow*, like *Captain from Castile* and *Desiree*, covers only the first two thirds of the novel. When Stephen and Odalie reconcile, the movie story ends. In the book Odalie dies giving birth to a stillborn child. Since Harrow plantation no longer has a mistress, Aurore moves in to help Stephen run the place. It doesn't take long before he discovers that she has always loved him. He grows to love her in return and they marry…and the story continues from there through the Civil War and beyond.

During his unhappy experience filming *The Foxes of Harrow*, Rex Harrison had consoled himself by having an extra marital affair with Carole Landis who was also a Fox contract player. Their affair lasted a year. On July 5, 1948, Carole took her own life. She was distraught over

Handsome heel Rex Harrison

Harrison's refusal to leave his wife and his impending departure for New York to appear in a play. Harrison and Carole's maid Fannie Mae Bolden discovered the body. Bolden later said that Harrison told her he would inform the proper people but instead "He didn't call the coroner, the police, or anybody. He just walked out."

Not long after Carole's funeral, Harrison bought himself out of his Fox contract and went to New York to appear in the play *Anne of the Thousand Days*. While the play was in tryouts in Philadelphia, Harrison gave an interview saying "So far as I am concerned Hollywood is done with. It took me three years to find out I don't like anything about it. It is so egocentric it doesn't know the rest of the world exists" (pot meet kettle). Needless to say, Hollywood took offense at his attitude and Hedda Hopper reported that "Rex Harrison's career is dead as a mackerel." His comments and the tragic affair with Carole Landis closed the door on his Hollywood career for the time being and during the next several years Harrison concentrated on stage performances in New York and London. Hollywood eventually forgave Rex Harrison but his reputation as a womanizing cad endured. To this day the Landis family believes that Harrison murdered Carole to avoid further scandal regarding their affair.

6

Captain From Castille
by Samuel Shellabarger

"Oh my senor, I love you. I love you so much it hurts."
— *Catana*

SAMUEL SHELLABARGER (1888-1954) was one of the two most popular writers who worked in the historical fiction genre during the Forties and Fifties, the other being Thomas B. Costain. Orphaned as an infant, Shellabarger was brought up by his grandfather, with whom he extensively travelled the world. These travels inspired him to become a writer at an early age. He later said that his travels "have left a nostalgia for the past which has colored my historical writing."

Shellabarger graduated from Princeton University in 1909 with a B.A. and studied a year at Munich University. Upon his return to the U.S. he earned his PhD at Harvard. He served in the Intelligence Corps. during World War I. He met his future wife, Vivan Borg, on a trip to Sweden and they were wed in 1915. Shellabarger and his wife travelled back and forth between the U.S. and Europe over the next several years while he honed his skills as a writer of mystery stories using the pseudonyms of John Esteven or Peter Loring. Later, Shellabarger taught at Princeton University but still found time to write on a regular basis. Although much of his output at this time was mysteries, in 1935 he wrote a biography of Lord Chesterfield. He used the research for this book when he wrote his novel *Lord Vanity* many years later.

Tyrone Power and Jean Peters in *Captain from Castile*

When he was in his Fifties, Samuel Shellabarger decided that he would try his hand at historical fiction. For the next decade he devoted his writing exclusively to this genre, producing four immensely popular novels, three of which were optioned for filming by 20th Century-Fox.

The first of these novels is *Captain from Castile,* published by Little, Brown, and Co. in 1945. The book became an immediate success and was at the top of the best seller lists throughout 1945. His other works of historical fiction are *Prince of Foxes* (1947), *The King's Cavalier* (1950), and *Lord Vanity* (1953). Shellabarger died of a heart attack in March 1954 at the height of his literary success.

THE MOVIE

Once again, 20th Century-Fox beat other studios to the punch and bought the rights to Samuel Shellabarger's forthcoming novel, *Captain from Castile*, while it was still in galleys. They purchased the film rights in December 1944 for $100,000 and the novel was published at the beginning of 1945. Shortly thereafter, Rev. John J. Devlin, a Hollywood representative of the Catholic Legion of Decency, warned Fox that the story was not acceptable to the Catholic Church in its depiction of the Inquisition. John Tucker Battle was given the job of writing a treatment of the novel prior to writing the screenplay. On January 20, 1945, Darryl F. Zanuck sent him a memo stating: "I feel that if you do all the things you want to do in order to satisfy the Church and the Hays Office, we will have taken out of the book everything that makes it a best seller. You do not have to use the actual name "Inquisition." Give it some other name. Also, you do not have to mention the Catholic Church." Battle finished his treatment in February 1945, and then proceeded to write a screenplay in collaboration with Samuel G. Engel.

On March 24, 1945, around the time the novel went into its 12th printing, Hedda Hopper stated, "Mighty smart of Darryl Zanuck to let Harry Cohen build Cornel Wilde up in three Technicolor pictures [at Columbia]. Now Darryl will star Wilde in *Captain from Castile*. And while getting this information, Cornel received word that he had been voted one of the 10 most popular actors in a fan magazine poll."

John Tucker Battle and Samuel Engel turned in their script in May 1945 but it was rejected by Zanuck. He quickly engaged Joseph L. Mankiewicz to write another treatment and to be a consultant on the project. On July 16, 1945, Mankiewicz wrote to Zanuck saying, "To do this picture ambitiously will cost a great deal of money. It will require Technicolor, a huge cast, great numbers of people, elaborate sets, costumes, props, locations, etc. The script will take a long time to write- thorough research will be necessary. Censorship problems should not be too difficult, once a satisfactory substitute for the Inquisition is established." Mankiewicz also suggested that Tyrone Power and Linda

Darnell should play the leads, Pedro de Vargas and Catana respectively, with Frederic March as Cortez.

It is hard to imagine that Zanuck didn't purchase the rights to *Captain from Castile* without Tyrone Power in mind for the lead. Perhaps Hedda Hopper was merely speculating when she mentioned Cornel Wilde. In a November 14, 1945 memo to George Cukor, who was set to direct *The*

Tyrone Power as Pedro de Vargas

Razor's Edge for Fox (he didn't), Zanuck said production on *Captain from Castile* would be pushed back for an entire year if necessary because the lead had been promised to Tyrone Power and he felt obliged to honor that commitment. In the meantime, Lamar Trotti, who would produce *Captain from Castile*, tackled the script and, following a research jaunt to Mexico, eventually produced a draft that satisfied both Zanuck and the Catholic Legion of Decency. To appease the Catholic Church, Trotti eliminated the character of Ingnacio de Lora, a corrupt priest and leader of the Inquisition in the book. Trotti said of his script, "Only one-third of the story represents action suitable for picturization. The screen version must omit everything that is not absolutely essential to the plot." Actually, Trotti's script represents the first two-thirds of the novel and ignores the last third entirely.

On December 14, 1945, Louella Parson's announced, "I hear through the grapevine that Linda Darnell gets the opportunity of a lifetime. She plays Cantana in *Captain from Castile*, opposite Tyrone Power. What a role! It's the part of the year. There is such adventure and color and Catana is nearly as vivid as Ty's role as the captain. After *Fallen Angel*, Linda was a cinch." In *Hollywood Beauty*, Ronald Davis' biography of Linda Darnell, he says, "[Linda] felt that the part would give her a chance to make her strongest impact yet, and she looked forward to the picture, convinced it would be her masterpiece." But the start of filming was a long way off and a lot would happen before the cameras turned.

With *The Razor's Edge* completed and set for release on Christmas Day 1946, Darryl Zanuck felt that the production of *Captain from Castile* could finally move into high gear. Ray Klune, Fox's Executive Production Manager, had already spent time in Mexico City in the summer of 1946. During this trip he hired Dr. Leopoldo Martinez Cosio from the Mexican National Museum to serve as a consultant and technical advisor on *Captain from Castile*. Also that summer, Henry King, who would be directing the film, flew his private plane around Mexico scouting locations. In 1933, King had visited Morelia, one of the Mexican Colonial cities. When he and Zanuck were discussing *Captain from Castile*, King told his boss "Darryl, I have a location in mind that I want to go look at. I think I know a town that will just fit what we are looking for." Zanuck replied, "Henry, how in the world is it that every time a picture comes up you know exactly where you're going to make it?"

While the logistics of filming a huge production like *Captain from Castile* in Mexico were being worked out, there were problems on another part of the Fox lot. *Forever Amber* had been shut down and the leading lady and director were to be replaced before filming would resume. Having previously tested just about every actress in Hollywood and England for the part of Amber, Zanuck now looked among his contract stars and decided Linda Darnell would be perfect in the part. Hedda Hopper made the official announcement on July 25, 1946: "Linda Darnell got the green light yesterday for the role of Amber." Linda Darnell was stunned by Zanuck's decision. She said, "I was practically living and breathing Catana when I got word I was to play the new Amber. Naturally it was the most thrilling surprise that has ever come to me. I thought I was the luckiest girl in Hollywood." It was quite a coup for Darnell who went from being the leading lady in a Tyrone Power picture to starring in one of the hottest properties in Hollywood.

Hedda Hopper ran a lengthy bit about *Captain from Castile* in her August 31, 1946 column:

> "Henry King, flying his own plane, found the ideal location for *Captain from Castile*. It's Morelia, 140 miles north of Mexico City, whose pure Spanish architecture has not been changed since the town was built in 1571. Two or three thousand of the city's 30,000 inhabitants will work in the picture, which King hopes to begin shooting not later than December. Linda Darnell is still begging Henry to save her role for which she was set until she finishes *Amber*. But I believe Paulette Goddard will get it. Tyrone Power wants her; and he usually gets what he wants."

Perhaps Power wanted Paulette Goddard but Zanuck wanted Jennifer Jones to play Catana. Zanuck had contacted producer David O. Selznick, who was Jennifer Jones' husband, and attempted to secure her for the role. Fox was owed a picture by Jones as part of a prior deal but Selznick wanted Zanuck to surrender that commitment to MGM so his wife could star in *Cass Timberlane*. In a September 20, 1946 memo to Selznick, Zanuck said, "I regret that Jennifer was not available for *Captain from Castile* as the role in the final version of the script has turned out superb. Henry King is directing and I am personally supervising the picture with Lamar Trotti as my associate. It is a $4,3000,000 subject and will probably be one of the great productions of next year. I still have not cast the role of Catana and if there is any change in your plans please telephone me at once."

Cesar Romero as Hernan Cortez

Cesar Romero had been a valued character actor at 20th Century-Fox since he signed his first contract there in 1937. Romero had been off the screen since 1943, when he enlisted in the U.S. Coast Guard during World War II. His first film following his tour of duty was in *Carnival in Costa Rica* after which Zanuck personally selected him to play Hernan Cortez in *Captain from Castile*. This would be the best dramatic part in the biggest film of Romero's career. It was great news for Tyrone Power as he and Romero were close friends and flying buddies.

The movie was back in Hedda Hopper's column on September 26, 1946: "It now comes out that Tyrone Power and Cesar Romero aren't jaunting over South America merely for pleasure. Ty's scouting locations for *El Conquistador*, a film he'll do with Henry King. The story, dealing with a soldier in the army of Simon Bolivar, is being prepared by Lamar Trotti. It's to be shot entirely in South America with all extra parts going to natives. Hollywood is more than anxious to strengthen its good neighbor policy in the western hemisphere. Two pictures, *Captain from Castile* with Ty Power, and *The Treasure of the Sierra Madre* with Humphrey Bogart, will be shot in Mexico in the autumn."

Louella Parsons reported on October 29, 1946 that Vincent Price had been cast as the "Spanish Inquisitor" in *Captain from Castile*. Parsons

John Sutton as Diego de Silva

was a bit premature with her news. Price refused to play the part of the villainous Diego de Silva, a decision which caused the actor to lose his contract at Fox. Price said de Silva was "the most despicable character I'd read…cruel actually for no reason except to make Tyrone Power look good. I refused to do it so they let my option drop." Price has an uncharacteristically narrow view of the character and his reasoning seems even more ridiculous when you consider the dastardly collection of villains he would eventually make his stock in trade. John Sutton ended up playing the part of Diego de Silva to perfection.

As the date to begin filming drew near, the part of Catana had still not been cast. Zanuck looked at all the screen tests that had been filmed and the only one that stood out had been made by a 19 year old girl from Ohio with no previous acting experience. Jean Peters had won the Ohio State Beauty Pageant in 1945 and the grand prize was a screen test at 20th Century-Fox. Henry King was not particularly interested in watching Peters screen test which basically showed her walking around in a bathing suit. Zanuck told him, "There's something about this girl, she's got something you might like." King watched her test and concurred that Jean Peters did have "something". He worked with her for two days and made further tests using what would be her most difficult scenes in *Captain from Castile*. After viewing these tests Zanuck told King, "This, in my estimation, is the most amazing thing I've ever seen in my life. Here's a girl who's never done anything in show business except walk around in a bathing suit. This girl is terrific." And thus Jean Peters was signed to a Fox contract and cast as Catana.

In early November 1946 a train left from Los Angeles bound for Mexico City. Eight baggage cars were filled with costumes, props, film equipment, and refrigerated Technicolor film stock to be used in the making of *Captain from Castile*. All of this was then transported by trucks to Morelia, which would double for 16th Century Spain in the early parts of the movie. Filming commenced in Morelia on November 19 and continued there for six weeks. There were four primary locations used: Morelia; Patzcuaro, located in the mountains east of Mexico City; the bay of Vera Cruz in Acapulco; and Uruapan, located seven miles from the active volcano Paricutin. Henry King had his production office set up in Uruapan throughout the shoot. Joseph LaShelle was originally hired as Director of Photography for the Mexico shoot but when he proved inexperienced with Technicolor location photography, Zanuck replaced him with Charles G. Clarke. Clarke shot the Mexico location footage,

Jean Peters as Catana

sometimes under the supervision of Second Unit Director Robert D. Webb. Later, Arthur E. Arling would take over as Director of Photography for the interiors shot in Hollywood. Filming progressed surprisingly well considering the scope of the production and the unpredictable weather but trouble soon appeared which would cause both 20th Century-Fox and MGM considerable consternation.

Prior to the start of filming *Captain from Castile*, Tyrone Power had formerly separated from his wife Annabella. He was introduced to Lana

Turner by Keenan Wynn's wife Evie and Power and Turner began a torrid love affair. When Power went to Mexico to film *Captain from Castile,* Lana Turner started work on MGM's multi-million dollar extravaganza *Green Dolphin Street.* Turner impulsively decided that she and Power should not be separated over New Year's Eve so, flaunting studio policy, she flew to Mexico City. She called Power, who was in Patzcuaro, and he sent a small plane to pick her up. Disaster struck when a tremendous rainstorm set in for two days and Turner could not fly back to Mexico City to catch a plane to Los Angeles. Filming on *Green Dolphin Street* was delayed, costing MGM thousands of dollars while the cast and crew waited for their star. Both Fox and MGM worried that the Power/Turner affair would generate bad publicity resulting in adverse public reaction toward the two stars and damage the prospects of their two costly productions.

Five weeks of filming were done at a thirty acre set constructed in Uruapan. Here the company had built an Aztec pyramid surrounded by a native huts. It was in this location that the most spectacular scene in the movie was filmed. Montezuma sends an envoy to Cortez in an attempt to convince the Spaniards to leave Mexico. This scene required 4,000 Mexican extras, all dressed in Aztec costumes and carrying weapons. It took three hours to dress the extras who were separated by the wardrobe people into groups of 800. Although this scene was filmed without a hitch, not long after a natural disaster would affect the Uruapan shoot of *Captain from Castile.*

The nearby Paricutin volcano erupted, filling the sky with smoke and ash, blocking out the sunlight, and preventing filming. This delay ended up costing the studio an estimated $27,000. However, the eruption did make for an impressive background for the last scene in the picture.

The last of the Mexican location shooting was done in Acapulco where, according to Louella Parsons, Lana Turner rented a house to be near Power. Tyrone Power met his future wife Linda Christian for the first time in Acapulco where she was filming *Tarzan and the Mermaids.* Ironically, Christian had just appeared with Turner in *Green Dolphin Street.* Lana Turner lost out in the end but always claimed that Tyrone Power was the love of her life.

The filming of *Captain from Castile* moved back to the studio in early March 1947 after 83 days of filming in Mexico. On March 27, Hedda Hopper reported one final bit of casting for the film, "Barbara Lawrence is another newcomer who is getting a break. This 16 year old

Tyrone Power and Barbara Lawrence

former Oklahoma girl will go into *Captain from Castile* as the fiancee of Tyrone Power. Barbara made her screen debut in *Margie*." All of Barbara Lawrence's scenes as the Lady Luisa de Carvajal were shot at the studio. Filming on *Captain from Castile* wrapped in April 1947. The shoot had lasted 106 days at a cost of $4,500,000. It was the only time Henry King ever went over schedule and over budget.

Alfred Newman wrote the background score for *Captain from Castile* and it is one of the finest ever composed for a motion picture. It would garner the film's only Academy Award nomination. The "Conquest" theme from Newman's score would later become the "Victory Song" played by the University of Southern California marching band at sports events.

Captain from Castile opened on Christmas Day 1947 at the Rivoli Theatre in New York City and Grauman's Chinese Theatre in Hollywood (where it played three weeks). Reviews were generally mediocre. *Variety* thought that "The coin poured into this production is visible in every inch of the footage" but complained that "There are several soft spots in the story that interfere with credibility." The unnamed *New York Times* critic said that readers of the novel "will be distressed to discover a rather pastel reflection of the book in 20th Century-Fox's film version." He also found the performances to be "indifferent". *Harrison's Reports* gave it a glowing review: "As a massive spectacle alone, this Technicolor production deserves high rating; but it has an interesting story as well, with plentiful action, considerable human interest, and a generous share of romance." The film went on to do good business at the box office but, like *Forever Amber*, the high cost of the production made it impossible for the picture to show a profit. *Captain from Castile* made $6 million worldwide but with the cost of promotion added to what had already been spent, the film ended up losing $2 million.

CAPTAIN FROM CASTILE
Released: December 1947. Running time: 140 minutes.
In Technicolor
Produced and Written by Lamar Trotti
Directed by Henry King
Music by Alfred Newman.
Cinematography by Charles G. Clarke and Arthur E. Arling
Edited by Barbara McLean.
Cast: Tyrone Power, Jean Peters, Cesar Romero, Lee J. Cobb, John Sutton, Antonio Moreno, Thomas Gomez, Alan Mowbray, Barbara Lawrence, George Zucco, Marc Lawrence

In Jaen, Spain in the year 1518 young Pedro de Vargas (Tyrone Power) incurs the enmity of the powerful Diego de Silva (John Sutton) when he allows Coatl (Jay Silverheels), a slave brought from Mexico, to escape. De Silva is the Supreme Justice of the Inquisition and he wastes no time in having Pedro and his family arrested for heresy. Pedro's 12 year old sister is tortured to death but he and his parents escape from prison. His mother and father decide to go to Italy to seek refuge with relatives there. Pedro, his imagination fired by stories of the fabulous riches of the Indies, joins the expedition of Hernan Cortez (Cesar Romero) and sets sail for the New World. With him are Juan Garcia (Lee J. Cobb) and Catana Perez (Jean Peters), friends who aided in his escape from prison.

In Mexico, Pedro discovers adventure, treachery, intrigue, and the steadfast love of Cantana. When Diego de Silva arrives in Mexico, bringing his evil cabal to the New World, Pedro's loyalty to Cortez is severely tested.

Catana Perez serves wine to Juan Garcia and Pedro de Vargas at the Rosario Inn

Pedro and Catana on a ship to the New World in a cut scene

Capt. Alvarado (Roy Roberts) arrests Pedro in a cut scene

As previously stated, the film version of *Captain from Castile* leaves out the last third of the novel. The movie ends on a seemingly triumphant note as Cortez and his Conquistadors march off to Tenochtitlan, the capital city of the Aztecs, where they will meet King Montezuma. In the novel, a bloody battle takes place there. Pedro and Catana are captured by the Aztecs and condemned to death. Coatl, the slave Pedro helped escape back in Spain, frees them and they eventually return to Spain where Pedro's family has been cleared of the charge of heresy.

One of the most fascinating characters in *Captain from Castile* is Dona Marina, played by the famous Mexican actress Estela Inda. In the film, Dona Marina is the interpreter for Cortez but in real life she was also his mistress. She gave birth to his son who was one of the first Mestizos, a person of mixed European and Indian blood. Sometimes revered but often reviled, Dona Marina later became known in Mexico as "La Malinche", meaning "a traitor to her country". In the movie, Estela Inda wears the actual necklace that Cortez gave to Dona Marina. It was on loan from the Chapultepec Castle museum in Mexico City.

Cortez scoffs at Cacamatzin (Ramon Sanchez), nephew of Montezuma, as Dona Marina (Estela Inda) and Coatl (Jay Silverheels) look on

Catana comforts Pedro who is about to be executed for the murder of Diego de Silva

Captain from Castile and I go back a long way. I can perfectly remember the circumstances of when I first saw it. It was mid-June 1961 and the day of my 6th grade graduation ceremony. I would now leave grammar school and start junior high school in September. Unfortunately it was also the day I came down with Chickenpox and was too sick to attend the ceremony. My last act, before being consigned to the darkness of my bedroom for the next week, was to watch the local afternoon movie, which happened to be *Captain from Castile*. It was the first time I ever saw Tyrone Power. I've been a fan of him and the film ever since.

Tyrone Power in *Prince of Foxes*

7

Prince of Foxes
by Samuel Shellabarger

"Women are the gage of a man's weakness."
– *Cesare Borgia*

AUTHOR SAMUEL SHELLABARGER had scored a tremendous success with *Captain from Castile* and he hit the jackpot again with his next delve into historical fiction. *Prince of Foxes* was published by Little, Brown and Company on July 14, 1947 and, like its predecessor, became an immediate bestseller. The novel, set during the Italian Renaissance, tells the story of Andrea Orsini, a clever and ambitious young man in the employ of Cesare Borgia. A few months after *Prince of Foxes* came out, Knopf Publishers released *Web of Lucifer: A Novel of Borgia Fury* by Maurice Samuel. This book also has as its central figure a resourceful youth employed by the Borgias. His name is Orso. Coincidence? Not likely. The book, however, was quickly forgotten and the author became better known for his various treatise on Judaism rather than his historical fiction.

THE MOVIE

20th Century-Fox optioned the rights to Samuel Shellabarger's forthcoming novel *Prince of Foxes* on May 18, 1946, more than a year prior to its publication. This option cost the studio $15,000, with the proviso that the novel would be published by July 1, 1947. When the publication of the novel was delayed, Fox let their option lapse on July 2. Having just sunk a fortune into the film versions of *Forever Amber* and *Captain from Castile,* Darryl Zanuck was unprepared to invest the money required for *Prince of Foxes,* which he figured would be another costly production.

In early 1948, director Henry King was hospitalized for a back injury. While convalescing, King read the novel *Prince of Foxes* and contacted Zanuck, saying he would like to direct the film with Tyrone Power as the star. Zanuck replied, "I think it's a great idea. Unfortunately, we have let our option expire, but since you're enthusiastic about *Prince of Foxes,* we will renew it immediately." Zanuck was true to his word and Fox paid $125,000 for the rights to film *Prince of Foxes.* Another reason for Zanuck's change of heart was the ability to use Fox funds which had been frozen in Italian lire. This accounted for the decision to make the film on location in Italy.

On February 17, 1948, Hedda Hopper said: "Darryl Zanuck, who shelved several of his important stories when the British tax was announced, has started dusting them off for production. One of the yarns, *Down to the Sea in Ships,* will be Tyrone Power's next picture. Ty, who planned another plane jaunt after two pictures, will have to combine business with pleasure. He's also scheduled for *Prince of Foxes,* which will be shot entirely in Italy during the early summer. The cast, except for three principals, will all have Italian actors. Henry King, the director, goes to Florence next month to pick locations and Zanuck will join him in Italy to check the backgrounds."

Zanuck didn't go to Italy as Hopper reported but he did send Henry King, cinematographer Leon Shamroy, and Second Unit Director Robert D. Webb to scout locations there. King hired an airplane and pilot in Rome and they searched for a walled city in good enough condition for filming. They found it at Mount Titano Castle in the Republic of San Marino, a sovereign state located on the Italian Peninsula. Henry King said: "Leon Shamroy and I photographed a lot of the locations in 16mm color, and it seemed that we got too much detail in the very places we didn't want it- the old buildings looked like ruins." The decision was made to shoot the movie in black and white. King felt that producer Sol Siegel sold Zanuck on the idea of shooting in black and white to save money but Leon Shamroy reluctantly agreed that many of the locations would probably photograph poorly in color. Shamroy's camera assistant on the picture was Giuseppe Rotunno who would later go on to become one of the most famous Italian cinematographers, working with such directors as Federico Fellini, Vittorio de Sica, and Luchino Visconti.

Wanda Hendrix as Camilla Verano

Meanwhile, back in Hollywood, the film was being cast. Tyrone Power was a given for the lead role of Andrea Orsini. In June 1948, Fox made a deal with Paramount to loan contract player Victor Mature, whom Cecil B. DeMille wanted for *Samson and Delilah*, in exchange for Paramount contract player Wanda Hendrix. Hendrix was a relative newcomer to Hollywood who was, at the time, best known for being Audie Murphy's girlfriend. She would play Camilla Verano, the object of Power's affections in the film. Once again Hedda Hopper was wrong when she said that all but the three principal roles would be played by Italians. The only Italian who plays a significant role in *Prince of Foxes* is the beautiful Marina Berti who was cast as Angela Borgia.

Both Zanuck and Henry King agreed that Orson Welles would be perfect for the part of Cesare Borgia. When he arrived in Rome, King

Orson Welles as Cesare Borgia

made two appointments to meet Welles, who was also in Rome, but Welles didn't show up for either of them. King was testing another actor for the part when Zanuck came to Rome with Charles K. Feldman, who was Welles' agent. Henry King had expected some difficulties with Orson Welles, having heard that the actor was temperamental and often ignored shooting schedules. He voiced his concerns to Feldman who replied, "He'll do anything you want. I'll guarantee that because he wants [*Prince of Foxes*] more than anything in the world. Furthermore, he needs the money." Feldman made sure Welles showed up to meet King for their next appointment and he was cast as Cesare Borgia, with the irresistible lure of a $100,000 paycheck. Welles would use this money to help finance his motion picture version of *Othello*.

Although Henry King found Orson Welles to be "very pompous" he turned out to be quite reliable and very interested in the overall production. In fact, Welles showed up on the set at 8 a.m. every morning whether he was needed or not. The director and actor would have only one disagreement. While shooting one of the crowd scenes Welles did not feel the extras were showing the proper deference and respect his character deserved. Henry King's response was, "Dear friend, you're getting more than you deserve. Just go on with the scene." There were no problems after this, although throughout the filming Welles gave acting tips on various scenes to Tyrone Power without the knowledge of the director.

The 110 day proposed shooting schedule commenced in November 1948 in Florence. Upon arrival, the cast and crew were met by a delegation of managers from all the city's cinemas in addition to actors, actresses, and opera stars from all of Florence's theatrical venues. Church bells were rung in greeting and there was a great display of fireworks. Filming on *Prince of Foxes* would also include locations in Siena, San Gimignano, and Venice.

During the shooting of some of the interiors for *Prince of Foxes* at Cinecitta Studios in Rome, Danny Kaye visited the set and decided to play a joke on Darryl Zanuck. He got into costume and played the part of a messenger in a scene with Power and Welles, who went along with the gag. Later, when Zanuck was viewing the rushes in his Palm Springs home with friend Clifton Webb, Webb suddenly exclaimed, "It couldn't be, but that guy looks like Danny Kaye." Zanuck ran the rushes again and indeed it was Danny Kaye. Zanuck sent the scene to Kaye for Christmas. He should have included a bill for the money wasted when the scene was reshot.

Tyrone Power and Henry King (with pipe) on location

Romance was also in the air while *Prince of Foxes* was shooting in Rome. On August 4, 1948, Audie Murphy visited Wanda Hendrix in The Eternal City and presented her with a diamond engagement ring. The couple wed in December back in Hollywood. While filming *Prince of Foxes*, Tyrone Power's divorce from his first wife, Annabella, became final. Power and his fiancee, actress Linda Christian, decided to marry in Rome. The couple wanted the ceremony to be held at Santa Francesca Romana church but a wedding had never been held there so they had to obtain special permission. The wedding took place on January 27, 1949 and it was, as Power biographer Fred Lawrence Guiles states, "the biggest thing of its kind in the history of modern Rome." Only the naming of a new Pope would garner more media attention. And speaking of Popes, Power and his new wife received a papal blessing from Pope Pius XII who said, "I am happy you have chosen my country for your wedding. The people love you here. The eyes of the world are upon you."

During the long shoot, production manager Booth McCracken suffered a heart attack and died December 3, 1948 in Rome. He had worked at Fox since 1932 and was only forty-three years old. Filming was completed at a cost of $4.5 million, half of which was paid with the frozen Italian lire funds. Originally Fox had intended to give *Prince of Foxes* a summer 1949 release but the date was pushed back until December 1949. The release was preceded by a publicity campaign costing $300,000. *Prince of Foxes* had its world premiere on December 9, 1949 at Grauman's Chinese Theatre in Hollywood where it played two and a half weeks. It opened at the Roxy Theatre in New York on December 23. Critic Bosley Crowther found it to be "A picture of stately magnificence" but he felt that "curiously missing from this picture is the believable breath of life and the sense of momentum and excitement that a story of the Renaissance should have." *Variety,* which was usually generous, found *Prince of Foxes* to be "slow and plodding in its exposition and execution" and that "Wanda Hendrix gives the weakest of the performances." Louella Parsons overcame her longstanding loathing of Welles and said "This is awesome Orson at his best."

The fact that it was not shot in color definitely hurt the prospects of *Prince of Foxes*. Henry King said, "It was one of those economical mistakes that costs you in the end. The picture did well, made money and all that, but at the same time, a picture of that kind just screams for color." Bosley Crowther agreed: "Technicolor, which is strangely lacking, might have helped the dramatic shortcomings of this picture." Audiences polled during previews had felt the same way. Nevertheless, Leon Shamroy's stunning black and white photography was nominated for an Academy Award, as was Vittorio Nino Novarese's costume design.

When *Prince of Foxes* opened in London, Fox reacted to the recently levied tax on American movies by refusing to allow any British made

Andrea Orsini shows Alfonso a portrait of Lucrezia Borgia

Count Marc Antonio Verano and his wife Camilla

been to him. Cesare resumes his attack on the city but offers to spare the place from total destruction if he is given Orsini as a prisoner. Carmilla refuses his offer but Orsini gives himself up. Cesare rides triumphantly into the city but help from an unexpected source frees Orsini from Cesare's clutches. Lead by Orsini, the people of Citta del Monte rise up against the troops of the usurper. Their revolt is the first step in what will eventually lead to Borgia's downfall…and a happy ending for Orsini and Carmilla.

The middle section of the novel is eliminated in the film adaptation. There are four parts and only the first and last are utilized for the screenplay. In the unused portions, the Duke d'Este sends Andrea Orsini to Viterbo to kidnap their local saint, Sister Lucia, and bring her to Ferrara. After accomplishing this task, Orsini goes to Rome where he becomes further involved with the intrigues of the Borgias, particularly

Camilla and Andrea Orsini

Marina Berti as Angela Borgia with Tyrone Power and Orson Welles

Angela, who attempts to kill him. None of this is in the film, which concentrates mainly on Orsini's time in Citta del Monte in the fourth part of the book.

Reading the novel *Prince of Foxes* and then comparing it to the motion picture gave me a further appreciation of how screenwriters can keep the essentials but tweak them to fit the demands of a screen version. In the first chapter of *Prince of Foxes* Andrea Orsini reveals that he is being sent to Ferrara by Cesare Borgia. Borgia is often talked about but his character doesn't actually appear in the book until page 233. Then he is described thusly, " Andrea Orsini, who had long studied him, conjectured that the mainspring of Borgia's nature was an egotism so intense as to be almost passionless, except for scorn of scruples and shortsightedness." A bit of typecasting here if you've ever read anything about Orson Welles. Unlike the novel, in the movie Cesare is introduced in the opening scene during the funeral of Lucrezia Borgia's husband. This is obviously far earlier than he would have appeared in a straightforward adaptation of the novel. The movie gets Orson Welles into the picture right away and he is given a lot of screen time. This is definitely a good thing as Welles gives a dynamic and memorable performance, served with just the right amount of "ham".

Tyrone Power and Cecile Aubrey in *The Black Rose*

8

The Black Rose
by Thomas B. Costain

"They can have their England. I'll not set foot on Norman soil."

– Walter of Gurnie

BORN IN BRANTFORD, Ontario, Canada, Thomas B. Costain (1885-1965), caught the writing bug at an early age. While still in high school he wrote four novels, all of which were rejected by publishers. He was hired as a reporter for the *Brantford Courier* in 1902 and his first published work was a story for that paper. He became an editor for the newspaper *Guelph Daily Mercury* in 1908. In 1910 Costain married and took his wife to Toronto where he worked as a writer and editor for *Maclean's Magazine*. In 1920, Costain moved with his wife and two children to New York City where he took the job of Chief Associate Editor for *The Saturday Evening Post*. He occupied this position for fourteen years and during this time became a U.S. citizen.

In 1934 Costain became the head of the story department for the New York branch of the Fox Film Corporation and held this post for two years. After a failed attempt at founding his own magazine, Costain signed on as the Advisory Editor with Doubleday and Company in 1939. He continued to write novels but felt none of them were good enough to submit to publishers. In 1942 Costain had his first book published. Titled *For My Great Folly*, it is a fictionalized account of the 17th century Barbary pirate Jack Ward, who would later inspire the character of Jack Sparrow in the Disney *Pirates of the Caribbean* movies. The novel became a best seller.

The *Black Rose* was Costain's fourth novel and it turned out to be his most successful. Costain claimed that the inspiration for the main character, Walter of Gurnie, was Gilbert Becket, the father of Thomas Becket. The book was published by Doubleday and Company in 1945. The first printing was 650,000 copies, which quickly sold out. *The Black Rose* became a selection of the Literary Guild in September 1945 and went on to sell over 2 million copies the first year. The success of *The Black Rose* enabled Costain to retire from Doubleday in January 1946 and devote his time to writing. The research that Costain did for *The Black Rose* and his 1947 novel *The Moneyman* would lead to the writing of his great non-fiction historical series *The Plantagenets*.

The discovery in Antioch of a First Century silver chalice inspired Costain to write his 1952 novel *The Silver Chalice*. It tells the story of a an artist who is commissioned by the followers of Jesus to design a silver chalice to hold the cup from which Jesus drank at the Last Supper. The book was on the *New York Times* best seller list for 64 weeks and became the best selling novel of 1953. Warner Bros. optioned *The Silver Chalice* and produced the motion picture version in 1954. It featured the film debut of Paul Newman.

Thomas Costain's final novel was *The Last Love* in 1963. It is a story of Napoleon's exile on the island of St. Helena. There he meets an English girl named Betsy Balcome and she becomes his "last love." Costain died of a heart attack two years after the publication of this book. Despite the tremendous popularity of his novels, only *The Black Rose* and *The Silver Chalice* were made into movies.

THE MOVIE

In October 1945, 20th Century-Fox purchased the film rights to *The Black Rose* for $87,500. Richard Tregaskis, who had written the script for Fox's *Guadalcanal Diary,* was hired to write the screenplay. In April 1946 Tregaskis submitted his first draft to Darryl Zanuck and it was rejected. The project was then turned over to Talbot Jennings who provided the final screenplay. Jennings had recently co-authored the script for Fox's big hit *Anna and the King of Siam*. Louis D. Lighton, another *Anna and the King of Siam* alumnus, would be producer on *The Black Rose* and Henry Hathaway was set to direct.

Cornel Wilde

When Cornel Wilde became one of the highest paid stars on the Fox lot, Zanuck wanted to get the most out of his investment. He slated Wilde to star in *The Black Rose* while *Forever Amber* was still in production. After *Amber*, Wilde was immediately scheduled for another loan out to Columbia to star in *It Had to Be You* with Ginger Rogers. Wilde told columnist Bob Thomas that he didn't "know whether to take a vacation or a suspension" prior to beginning *The Black Rose*. Wilde wanted that time to finish a novel he was writing on Lord Byron.

On February 25 1947, Peggy Cummins was mentioned in Hedda Hopper's column as the possible "feminine lead" of *The Black Rose*. This was confirmed by Sheila Graham in her June 14, 1947 gossip column: "Peggy Cummins is preparing for her third picture since she relinquished the role of Amber in *Forever Amber*. With one picture in theaters, *The Late George Apley,* a second about to be released in June, *Moss Rose,* and

Peggy Cummins

a third, *The Black Rose*, due to start production, Peggy's cancelled Amber role may prove to be the best thing that could have happened to her- especially as *Amber* won't be released until November. In *The Black Rose*, Peggy's co-star is Cornel Wilde- and she marries him in the fadeout. This puts her one up on Linda Darnell, who loses Cornel in *Forever Amber*. Peggy plays a half-Mongolian, and for a third of the picture she's a boy. Peggy, who is very blonde, will probably wear a black wig for *The Black Rose*- unless they change the title to *The Blonde Rose*."

With the two leads confirmed, *The Black Rose* was set to start filming in July 1947 with an estimated budget of $3,200,000. The start date of production came and went but on August 31, 1947 Hedda Hopper was optimistic: "Still looks as if Cornel Wilde, Henry Hathaway and Buddy Lighton will be the talented trio to do *The Black Rose*." Shortly thereafter it was announced by Fox that production on *The Black Rose* would be delayed indefinitely.

On October 10, 1947, *Daily Variety* published the following article:

> AMBER, CASTILE USHER OUT BIG COIN SPECTACLES
>
> "Looks now as if King Charles II and the Spanish conquistadores are ushering out the heavy- dough costumers in Hollywood. Check-up yesterday showed very little, if any, box car figure, spectacular production coming up after 20th-Fox's *Captain from Castile*, now finished and waiting release.
>
> This one and *Forever Amber* will be 20th-Fox's last venture into expensive spectacle field for some time. Studio shelved Thomas Costain's novel *The Black Rose*, a story which would out-glamor them all on the screen and would run well into the multi-million production brackets, because they felt cost was not justified now. Cornel Wilde was set to star."

Producer Louis D. Lighton said that production costs had increased 33% and box office returns had decreased. The studio had already invested $200,000 in development of *The Black Rose* but it was decided to shelve the project until the box office prospects had improved. Not mentioned by Lighton was the 75 % tax which had recently been imposed by England on the profits of Hollywood films showing in that country. This was a tremendous blow to Hollywood studios as England supplied about 34% of the revenue for their product.

Cornel Wilde got his wish for a vacation after all and took his wife, actress Patricia Knight, to Hawaii. When he returned he was cast by Fox in *The Walls of Jericho*, a story of small town scandal. Peggy Cummins went to work in the third installment of Fox's *My Friend Flicka* series, *Green Grass of Wyoming*.

In December 1948, Zanuck decided to take *The Black Rose* out of mothballs and film it abroad, once again using Fox funds which were frozen in Europe after the war. Gregory Peck was mentioned for the lead but Zanuck decided to go with his reliable swashbuckler Tyrone Power. The plan was for Power to stay in Italy once filming on *Prince of Foxes* had finished and begin filming *The Black Rose* there in March 1949. Cornel Wilde was in New York when this news was announced and he immediately flew back to Hollywood to try and get back the part. Zanuck was adamant that Power would star. Fox attempted to sign Leslie Caron to play opposite Power. There are conflicting reasons as to why she didn't. One version says her mother did not approve of the script but Leslie Caron told Hedda Hopper in 1953: "I never wanted to be an actress, although my mother suggested it instead of my being a dancer. I refused the part in *The Black Rose* because I didn't want to be in pictures."

In March 1949, *Daily Variety* announced that *The Black Rose* would start filming in Morocco on April 18, 1949. On April 5, Hedda Hopper ran the following blurb: "Big Break- Cecile Aubry plays Tyrone Power's leading lady in *The Black Rose*. She's 18 and has done one picture only. She signed a long termer with 20th and will meet Ty in Casablanca for the start of the film."

Actually Cecile Aubry was 21 years old and had made two movies in her native France. Zanuck decided to re-team Power with Orson Welles, who would play the Mongol warlord, Bayan of the Hundred Eyes. The majority of the rest of the cast and crew would be British.

Location filming took place throughout Morocco, beginning in Marrakech where the company was housed at the Mamounian Hotel, then considered one of the most luxurious hotels in the world. The production then moved to an abandoned Foreign Legion outpost in Ouarzazate, where accommodations were not nearly so deluxe. In fact, when a bridge was washed out in a rainstorm, Tyrone Power and his wife Linda Christian, accompanied by co-star Jack Hawkins, got separated from the rest of the company and had to spend time in a remote ramshackle inn.

Jack Hawkins recounted the story in his autobiography *Anything for a Quiet Life*: "There was no turning back, for a tree had been uprooted behind us and blocked the road. So we sat with the rain driving on the car roof, and the river rising. Then I saw a face at the window. A man was standing outside. He explained to us he was a Russian who owned- of all things in that desolate place- a restaurant. We would be welcome to shelter there. We took him at his word and raced through the rain to a very rough-looking building, little better than a wooden shack. We dried our clothes in front of a stove, and he said, very kindly, that he would prepare a meal for us. The restaurant seemed a crude place and this prospect did not fill us with enthusiasm, so I was astonished by the magnificent dinner that arrived. Here we stayed for three days, living like peasants and eating like kings. And nobody knew we were there!"

Cecile Aubrey had a similar experience but it did not turn out as well. Caught in the same flash flood, Aubrey, her mother, and the driver of their car were stranded in the Atlas Mountains for three days without food before a rescue party could locate and save them.

Jack Hawkins (center) as Tristram Griffin and Tyrone Power as Walter of Gurnie in *The Black Rose*

Tyrone Power and Jack Hawkins bonded during the filming and remained close friends until Power's untimely death in 1958. Henry Hathaway had only the highest praise for Power, whom he felt was the "perfect star" who never complained and was always prepared to give his best. Hathaway did not feel the same way about Orson Welles and said that Welles tended to play his part "every way except the way I told [him] to do it." Cinematographer Jack Cardiff recalled an incident in which Welles refused to recite a lengthy speech straight through. He continually, and deliberately, fluffed his lines. Hathaway refused to give in and after the thirty-sixth take Welles, near collapse, finally gave in and delivered the speech without a single error. As with Henry King on *Prince of Foxes*,

Orson Welles as Bayan of the Hundred Eyes

Hathaway had to stand his ground with Welles. One of Orson Welles' costumes as Bayan of the Hundred Eyes was a heavy Russian leather cloak with a mink lining. Wearing this cloak in the 120 degree heat of the Moroccan desert was an ordeal but Welles endured the discomfort. Jack Cardiff reported that after Orson Welles finished filming his part he departed "with the company's mink coat and a few cans of unexposed negative film which would be useful on *Othello*."

Jack Hawkins felt that Henry Hathaway was "an extraordinary man" who "had a sharp tongue and fired people at the drop of a hat." When Hawkins and Hathaway got in an argument early on, the actor told his director "All right, get someone else to play the part. I'll go home, I could not give a damn." They got on fine after that. Jack Hawkins was not fond of his role in *The Black Rose*. He considered it "a boring part" and said, "I don't know why I was cast for the role. It was a Tony Curtis part- before the arrival of Tony Curtis." Okay Jack, if you say so.

When location filming finished in Morocco, the company moved to England where interiors were shot at London Studios, Shepperton. Further location work would be done at Warwick Castle in Warwickshire, England. As filming drew to an end, Tyrone Power sent his friend Clifton Webb a postcard with a photo of a boar's head with an apple in its mouth on a silver platter. On the back he wrote, "I'll be home on the 15th. As you can see, I ran into [society hostess] Elsa Maxwell over here and she's in fine fettle. Ty."

The 20th Century-Fox studio newsletter *Dynamo* announced the completion of the film to Fox employees: "After three years of preparation and six months of filming, the eagerly-awaited picturization of Thomas B. Costain's best-selling novel *The Black Rose* has been completed- at a cost approximating four-million dollars. More than 17,000 people on three continents will have had a hand in transferring this moving story to the screens of the world. It has been filmed entirely in Technicolor."

On September 1, 1950 *The Black Rose* had simultaneous premieres at Grauman's Chinese Theatre in Hollywood and at the Roxy Theatre in New York City. A week later the movie had its London premiere at the Odeon Leichester Square with Cecile Aubry in attendance. It would be Mademoiselle Aubry's only English language motion picture. She married a son of the Pasha of Marrakech and retired from acting in 1959. She later earned considerable fame in France as a writer of children's books.

Despite all of Fox's best efforts in making *The Black Rose*, reviews were fair to poor. *Variety* said, "In a picture of warring, there is only the suggestion of battle. Perhaps one good scene, with some honest-to-goodness cinematic bloodletting might have done something to increase the tempo of the picture. Power is credible in the lead role, while Welles underplays effectively." *New York Times* critic Bosley Crowther for once seemed reluctant to heap his usual bile on the movie version: "The motion picture drama which Talbot Jennings has digested from the book is a woefully unexciting account of gaudy but static episodes. Somehow or other, Mr. Jennings managed to twist and skirt around virtually every dynamic encounter of any large and lusty consequence in the book. This is a painful estimation for a reviewer to have to make of a film based on such a popular novel." John McCarten at *The New Yorker* was just plain nasty: "*The Black Rose* is a massive coagulation of overblown dialogue, preposterous acting, drooling Technicolor, and dubious history." *Time* said "Actor Welles proves surprisingly convincing as the tough Mongol general."

The Black Rose made $2.65 million at the U.S. box office and performed very well overseas, particularly in England. It was nominated for an Academy Award for Best Color Costume Design.

THE BLACK ROSE
Released: September 1950. Running time: 120 minutes
In Technicolor
Produced by Louis D. Leighton
Directed by Henry Hathaway
Screenplay by Talbot Jennings.
Music by Richard Addinsell
Cinematography by Jack Cardiff
Edited by Manuel Del Campo.
Cast: Tyrone Power, Cecile Aubry, Orson Welles, Jack Hawkins, Finley Currie, Herbert Lom, Alfonso Bedoya, Mary Clare, James Robertson Justice, Gibb McLaughlin

In 13th Century England, Walter of Gurnie (Tyrone Power) is the illegitimate son of a Saxon nobleman who has married a Norman woman. When his father dies, Walter makes a scene at the reading of the will but is saved from arrest by the intervention of the Norman king, Edward

(Michael Rennie). When Walter and his boyhood friend Tristram Griffin (Jack Hawkins) help to free some Saxon prisoners, they must flee England or face imprisonment themselves.

Seeking adventure, the two men journey to far off Cathay. There they join forces with the fierce Mongol warlord Bayan of the Hundred Eyes (Orson Welles) who is leading a caravan transporting women and riches to the great Kubla Khan. One of the women is Maryam (Cecile Aubry), a half English girl who is known as "The Black Rose". She asks Walter

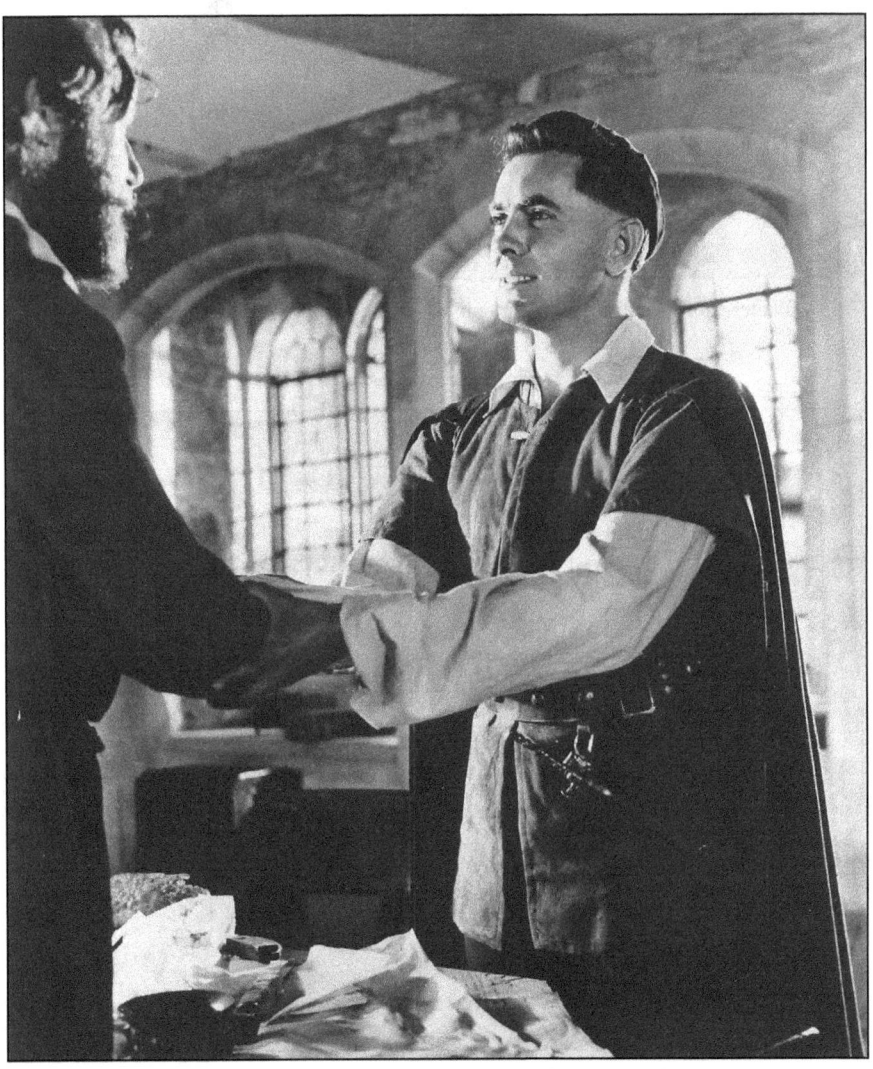

Walter is greeted by his friend Simeon (James Robertson Justice)

Walter shows Tristram and Maryam an invention of the Chinese…gunpowder

Walter and Maryam escape from the Chinese palace

and Tristram to give her their protection. Along the way, villages fall to Bayan's soldiers and innocent people are wantonly slaughtered. Walter falls in with Bayan's plans of conquest which will eventually take them to China, but Tristram is repulsed by all the bloodshed he has seen and flees from Bayan's caravan with Maryam. Walter is sent as a spy to the Empress of China (Madame Phang) but he is captured and kept a prisoner at the palace. There he finds that Tristram and Maryam are also prisoners.

The Empress believes a prophecy which says that two "white gods" will be China's only protection against invading armies. The Englishman are to be held indefinitely to insure this protection. Walter devises a plan of escape but Tristram dies in the attempt and Walter and Maryam, who have fallen in love, are separated. Walter returns to England where he presents King Edward with some printed books and other inventions he and Tristram had discovered in Cathay. His friend Tristram taught him the lesson that he must be "English first and Saxon second" and these inventions can advance the future his country. The King rewards him with a title which negates his illegitimacy. Bayan has found Maryam and sends her to Walter in England to repay the friendship Walter had shown him.

The supporting cast of British actors is one of the great attributes of *The Black Rose*. Many of the players would become familiar faces in the years to come. Although Jack Hawkins had been in British films since 1930, *The Black Rose* would be his biggest exposure thus far to American moviegoers. Laurence Harvey is also featured in an early supporting role in this film. Michael Rennie, in particular, benefited greatly from his appearance in *The Black Rose*. Already a star of some stature in England, this film would provide the boost he needed to gain international recognition.

Tyrone Power and Michael Rennie became friends during the filming and, upon his return to Hollywood, Power spoke to Darryl Zanuck about Rennie. Zanuck offered Rennie one of the main roles in Otto Preminger's *The 13th Letter*, which would be shot in Quebec. Zanuck was so impressed by Rennie's performance in this film that he offered him a long term contract. The first film under his Fox contract was *The Day the Earth Stood Still* in which he memorably starred as "Klaatu", a benevolent visitor from another planet. Fox gave him the leading role of Jean Valjean in their 1952 version of *Les Miserables* but when the movie failed to perform well

Michael Rennie as King Edward in *The Black Rose*

at the box office, Fox lost faith in Rennie as a leading man. For the rest of his time at the studio Rennie was cast in important supporting roles in some of Fox's biggest pictures. The last film under his Fox contract was *Island in the Sun* in 1957, although he would return to the studio for *The Lost World* in 1960.

A final note: The *American Film Institute Catalog* entry on *The Black Rose* states that Madame Phang's part as the "Empress of China" was entirely cut from the picture. This is not true. She features quite prominently in a scene with Tyrone Power.

William Marshall in *Lydia Bailey*

9

Lydia Bailey
by Kenneth Roberts

"You'll come back to us. We won't have much, but we'll have our freedom."

– King Dick

KENNETH ROBERTS (1885-1957) was a prolific writer of historical fiction. Two months before his death he received a Pulitzer Prize Special Citation for his contributions in the historical fiction genre dealing with early American history. He began his writing career as a journalist, first for the *Boston Post* and later as an the American correspondent in Europe for *Saturday Evening Post*. Friend and neighbor Booth Tarkington (author of *The Magnificent Ambersons*) convinced Kenneth Roberts to give up his career in journalism and try his hand at writing novels. Roberts' first novel *Arundel* (1929) deals with the American Revolution and most of his subsequent books would also be about various aspects of American history. However, *Lydia Bailey*, written in 1947, is about the Haitian Revolution during the 1800s led by the former slave Toussaint L'Ouventure. Napoleon sent his brother-in-law, General Charles Leclerc, to Haiti in 1802 to put down the rebellion and restore slavery.

One of the main characters in *Lydia Bailey* is "King Dick", whose real name was Richard Crafus. Born in Maryland, he went to Europe as a privateer during the war of 1812 and ended up imprisoned in 1814 at Dartmoor Prison in England. King Dick ruled over more than a thousand black prisoners incarcerated at Dartmoor where, according to one inmate, "His word was supreme." In this capacity King Dick appears in an earlier novel of Kenneth Roberts, *The Lively Lady* (1931).

When Kenneth Roberts first thought of writing *Lydia Bailey* in 1940, he realized that much of his research would be found in the manuscript *Voyage Aus Etats Unis d'Amerique 1793-1798* by Moreau de St. Mery. This work had been published in French in 1913 but no English translation existed. Roberts obtained the rights to the 400 page document and put the writing of *Lydia Bailey* on hold for six months while he translated the French manuscript into English with the help of his wife Anna. This translation was published as *American Journey* in 1947, the same year *Lydia Bailey* came out. *Lydia Bailey* was published by Doubleday & Company and became a huge success. The novel spent twelve weeks at the top of the *New York Times* best seller list in 1947. It had taken Roberts six years to complete the novel which he dedicated to *Leave Her to Heaven* author Ben Ames Williams: "To Ben Ames Williams in gratitude for patient assistance in a struggle that long seemed hopeless."

THE MOVIE

In September 1946, prior to the novel's publication, 20th Century-Fox paid $215,000 for a ten year option on *Lydia Bailey*. This purchase was based on Kenneth Roberts' reputation as an author and on a brief synopsis of the story. *Variety* touted this as "the biggest blind deal of its kind in industry history." Doubleday's attorney warned Roberts that "If you use any fictional characters in a subsequent book which have appeared in *Lydia Bailey*, it would be impossible to sell that book to anyone except 20th." The attorney goes on to say that because King Dick "was a real person, 20th will have no hold on him." Thus, if another company should choose to film *The Lively Lady*, Roberts could not be sued by Fox.

The next mention of a film version of *Lydia Bailey* was in Sheila Graham's "Hollywood Gadabout" column on June 1, 1947: "Linda Darnell will not be getting the long rest she says she wants. But she won't mind too much. Her next picture is *Lydia Bailey*, current best seller. It's the story of a raving beauty whom men go crazy about, and would seem right down Linda's alley. The picture goes into production at Fox in the fall." Over a year later, in a July 14, 1948 article by Hollywood journalist Bob Thomas, Darnell still wants a rest: "Linda Darnell has worked for a solid year and is telling 20th-Fox she'll take a vacation after [*A Letter to*] *Three Wives*. If the studio plans to star her in *Lydia Bailey*, it hasn't told her about it. At any rate, the film probably won't be made for years because of the expense."

This last statement is most likely in response to a cost conscious comment Darryl Zanuck made to Hedda Hopper in early October 1947 saying, "We've postponed many of our high-budget pictures- among them *Lydia Bailey, The Black Rose, Julie,* and *Down to the Sea in Ships*. In the future we'll use good ideas where we once used money lavishly. Elaborate scenes unnecessary to the picture will be eliminated."

On April 18, 1949, Sheila Graham reported that Italian star Rossano Brazzi was to star in *Lydia Bailey*, most likely opposite Linda Darnell in the title role. Another year went by and Hedda Hopper wrote in her

Susan Hayward

May 4, 1949 column that Zanuck had just signed Susan Hayward to a longterm Fox contract. Says Hedda, "I'm betting *Lydia Bailey* will be her first film there. The part, one of the most coveted on the lot, is that of a temperamental beautiful gal, which would be right down Susan's alley." Apparently Hollywood gossip columnists liked that "down alley" metaphor.

In June 1949, it was announced that Sol Siegel would be producing the film in Jamaica and England to utilize Fox frozen funds. By November 1950, Jules Schermer had replaced Sol Siegel as producer and French actress Micheline Prelle (aka Presle) would star as Lydia. Tyrone Power was announced as the male lead, Albion Hamlin in April 1951. Soon after, Micheline Prelle was out and Hedy Lamarr was being seriously considered for the title role. It was probably down her alley as well.

The Afro-American newspaper took great interest in the filming of *Lydia Bailey* and made several reports on the progress of the motion picture. An April 21, 1951 article entitled "*LYDIA BAILEY*- NEW FOX FILM TO HAVE MIXED CAST" waxes enthusiastically about the movie: "This movie promises to surpass all previous films in giving opportunity to colored talent." The article gives May 20, 1951 as the proposed start date of shooting, although Zanuck had still not found "a colored actor with both the stature and dramatic ability to create the all important role of King Dick." William Marshall had been approached but had to refuse the offer because of his commitment in the New York stage production of *Green Pastures*. The article goes on to say that Le Roi Antoine, a Haitian born concert artist, has been signed to a "lucrative contract" by Fox as the Technical Director. Antoine's credentials included a book he co-authored with his wife about the history of Haiti called *Soul of Haiti*. "Antoine will teach the actors portraying natives how to speak the French dialect of the island. He already has begun to teach a group of singers the Haitian songs, and he must also teach the dancers and coach the voodoo."

On May 26, 1951, *The Afro-American* ran the article "MARSHALL BEING FITTED FOR *LYDIA BAILEY* ROLE". It says, "William Marshall, dramatic star who made such a hit in the recent ill-fated stage version of *Green Pastures*, will fly to Hollywood to play King Dick in 20th Century-Fox's *Lydia Bailey*. He is now being fitted for his wardrobe in the new motion picture which will present a phase of Haitian history. This Technicolor film, which stars Tyrone Power, is scheduled to go before the cameras June 4. Acquisition of Marshall for the King Dick role finally ended a long nationwide search for an actor to play this part. Not until *Green Pastures* closed on Broadway could Marshall sign a contract with 20th Century-Fox."

On June 3, 1951, Louella Parson's announced: "ANNE FRANCIS GETS BIG ROLE WITH TYRONE IN *LYDIA BAILEY*"… "Still they keep coming. These brand-new, fresh personalities getting the breaks in the big picture. The latest is Anne Francis, debutante at 20th who will be in Ty Power's *Lydia Bailey*." Parson's was obviously a bit behind the times when she wrote this because at this point Tyrone Power had already quit the picture.

Three days after Louella Parson's "scoop", Bob Thomas wrote an article with the heading "HOLLYWOOD JOLTED BY STUDIO'S SUSPENSION OF TYRONE POWER". In it he says "The filmtown got a jolt last week when it learned that Tyrone Power had been suspended by his studio. For 15 years he had been the king of 20th Century-Fox. He was the fair-haired boy who could do no wrong. This was his first suspension. So I sought him out to ask how it all happened. 'The studio's announcement was correct', he declared. 'The hard fact is that I just can't do another costume picture.' He was cast in *Lydia Bailey* but declined the assignment. 'I've had enough costume pictures,' he continued. "I've done five in a row. That's too much for one actor. I think it's time I had a change of pace. You have to talk in a stilted kind of dialog,' he remarked. 'I'd like to do a picture in which I could talk as normal people talk.' The actor added that his dispute with the studio was a friendly one. 'They were very nice about it,' he explained. 'Still they had to suspend me as an example to the other players'". Power's next picture would be the post WWII espionage thriller *Diplomatic Courier*.

Errol Flynn was approached about replacing Power but when he sustained spinal injuries during a brawl in a Nassau, Bahamas nightclub, he was unable to take the part. Flynn sued Canadian millionaire Duncan McMartin for $223,200 in Bahamas Supreme Court, claiming that a "vicious blow" administered by McMartin has cost Flynn the part in *Lydia Bailey* for which he would have been paid $200,000. Flynn was eventually awarded only $14,000 for this mishap.

With the departure of Tyrone Power, the status of the film seemed to diminish. NAACP Secretary Walter White had urged Fox to shoot the film on location in Haiti to help boost tourism and provide much needed revenue there. Instead *Lydia Bailey* would be filmed on the Fox backlot and on the Fox Ranch in Calabasas, located about 25 miles from the studio. By 1950, Zanuck had decided that no film produced by Fox would cost more than $2 million.

On June 24, 1951 a syndicated article written by Harold Heffernan entitled "TIRED OLD FACES ARE ON THE WAY OUT" appeared in newspapers. Heffernan states that "Current problems at the box office are opening unparalleled opportunities for new, younger faces on the screen."

Dale Robertson as Albion Hamlin in *Lydia Bailey*

He cites Darryl Zanuck's new policy of casting relative unknowns in important productions: "His first step in that direction is the assignment of Anne Francis, brand new to films- although she has enjoyed some little success via television- in the title role of *Lydia Bailey,* an expensive color adaptation of Kenneth Roberts' best-selling novel. Opposite her will be another actor comparatively new to fans. He is Dale Robertson, who has had a couple of good supporting parts and is looked upon as a potential palpitator. Taking *Lydia Bailey* as an example, it's casting is a far cry from what was originally planned a few months ago. Robertson replaces Tyrone Power. Miss Francis succeeds to a role that was announced for either Linda Darnell or Hedy Lamarr."

Hedda Hopper interviewed Dale Robertson about his role in *Lydia Bailey* in October 1951. Robertson said, "A star role is a fine thing for an unknown if he makes good. It can operate the other way too. I understand Tyrone Power's refusal to play the part. I could see his point of view. He's an established star and the role is actually not the best part in the picture. The best role is that of King Dick- the part played by Bill Marshall. Nobody can top that. When a man has reached the stature of Ty Power, his part should be predominant." Robertson also praised his new boss, "I think Darryl Zanuck knows more about pictures than any man here. And I threw in my lot with him for less money, knowing it was the best personal investment."

Anne Francis did not have good memories of filming *Lydia Bailey.* She told interviewer Cork Millner, "I was completely wrong for the part. It should have been a flashy, dark-haired actress like Linda Darnell. I was much too blonde and much too young for the character." While Francis felt that co-star Dale Robertson was "an easygoing country boy who seemed to take the Hollywood scene completely in his stride," she was herself "unbearably homesick and frightened by the prospect of a seven-year stretch during which I would have no say in my career." She also received little support from her director Jean Negulesco. When she asked for some advice about her character during a scene, Negulesco said "You're an actress. Act!" In addition to the emotional stress she felt making the movie, Francis also suffered some physical setbacks. She fell off a horse while rehearsing a scene and had to use a cane when not on camera. She had an allergic reaction to the dark face makeup she wore for the scenes in which she poses as a native Haitian. And she had strep throat for much of the shooting. As Thelma Ritter says in *All About Eve,* "Everything but the bloodhounds snapping at her rear end."

Anne Francis as Lydia Bailey

The screenplay by Michael Blankfort and Philip Dunne focuses only on the portions of the book which are set in Haiti. In the second half of the novel Albion Hamlin goes to the Mediterranean coast of Tripoli and becomes involved in the first Barbary War between the United States, Sweden, and the North African Barbary States. Kenneth Roberts disliked what had been done to his novel. He thought that Blankfort and

Dunne were "tenth-raters and bush leaguers" who were unfit to "dabble in the arts." In 1940 MGM had made a film version of Kenneth Roberts' 1937 novel *Northwest Passage*. The film starred Spencer Tracy and dealt with only the first half of the novel. Roberts hated the movie and, at the time, resolved to sell no more of his books to Hollywood. Apparently the $215,000 Fox offered him for *Lydia Bailey* weakened his resolve.

Focusing on only one portion of a novel was a common practice in Hollywood whenever a lengthy book was translated into a screenplay. 20th Century-Fox screenwriters did it repeatedly. Many years later there was quite a fuss made when the 1966 United Artists movie version of James A. Michener's *Hawaii* used only material from the third chapter of the book which deals with the Christian missionaries. Readers who loved the book felt cheated. I can understand both points of view but if the tone of the book can be captured by the movie, it should still be considered some great measure of success.

Leaving out the second half of *Lydia Bailey* wasn't the only change wrought by the screen-writers. The character of King Dick was drastically altered. In a 2013 essay on Hollywood's representation of King Dick, writer Alan Thomas Lipke says that the character was rewritten to conform to "Hollywood formulae and movie cliches". According to Lipke, King Dick has been transformed from Kenneth Roberts' buffoonish "slave of the lamp" into a "noble master and patriot." He goes on to say that "Under the unself-conscious imperial gaze naturalized by Hollywood's dream factory, he becomes an American aristocrat, above the blood, sweat and toil of making a living." Basically Lipke believes that the character of King Dick has been turned into a white man. Lipke is judging the movie by the standards of the 21st century. The film was made long before "Political Correctness" became the order of the day. Lipke seems to be of the opinion that William Marshall is done a disservice by being saddled with this role, although the part is clearly the most important one in the picture and is written with great dignity. In fact all the black characters in *Lydia Bailey* are treated without condescension. For a movie made in the early 1950s, this is a minor miracle. Lipke derisively speculates that NAACP Secretary Walter White approved of Hollywood's transformation of King Dick, believing that black audiences "might pay to see a dignified black hero, but would not be interested in another demeaning clown-character." And why wouldn't Mr. White approve of that?

Walter White did successfully engineer the May 4, 1952 world premiere of the film in Port-au-Prince, Haiti. Anne Francis and William

Marshall attended the premiere which was followed by a reception and grand ball at the National Palace, hosted by Haiti's President Paul Magloire. The stars remained for a four day festival celebrating Haiti's 150th year of independence. During her time in Haiti, "Calamity Anne" suffered more mishaps in conjunction with *Lydia Bailey*. During a parade honoring the release of the film she fell off a horse and later she was kicked by a donkey while on a sightseeing tour. Upon her return to the United States she collapsed at LaGuardia Airport. Columnist Dorothy Kilgallen said "Doctors blamed it all on the strenuous week she just spent in Haiti. Anne had to attend two parades and four parties in addition to the opening night whoopie." *Lydia Bailey* had it's U.S. premiere in Baltimore, Maryland shortly thereafter. Walter White was later criticized for not having invited Haitian President Paul Magloire to attend.

A month after *Lydia Bailey* went into release, *The Afro-American* ran an article on June 17, 1952 under the heading "HAITIAN EXPERT DENIED CREDITS ON *LYDIA BAILEY*". It goes on to say, "One who did much to make the film *Lydia Bailey* the success it certainly is, and who did not receive one line of credit either on the screen or in the sheet cast

William Marshall as King Dick and Dale Robertson as Albion Hamlin

of characters and credits, was Le Roi Antoine. Mr. Antoine spent four months on the work and preparation of the art and technical assistance. He was present at the press preview of the picture and, after the showing, plainly showed traces of his great disappointment caused by the studio bosses not giving him credit for the fine and outstanding contribution made by him in the film. He had ample reasons to have been heartbroken at seeing others get credit for his fine work." Jack Cole gets the sole choreography credit for the voodoo sequence. Cole (in blackface!) and famed choreographer Alvin Alley appear in this scene as voodoo dancers.

LYDIA BAILEY

Released: May 1952. Running time: 89 minutes.
In Technicolor
Produced by Jules Schermer
Directed by Jean Negulesco
Screenplay by Michael Blankfort and Philip Dunne
Music by Hugo Friedhofer
Cinematography by Harry Jackson
Editing by Dorothy Spencer.
Cast: Dale Robertson, Anne Francis, William Marshall, Charles Corvin, Juanita Moore, Luis Van Rooten, Ken Renard, Roy E. Glenn, William Walker

In 1802, Alboin Hamlin (Dale Robertson), a lawyer from Baltimore, goes to Haiti to find Lydia Bailey (Anne Francis). She is the daughter of a deceased client and Hamlin must get her signature on a document in order to obtain the rich estate which is bequeathed to the United States government in her father's will. No sooner does Hamlin arrive in Haiti's port city Cap Francois than his young black porter is stabbed to death by two white men who are trying to steal Hamlin's luggage. A black man comes to Hamlin's aid and explains that it dangerous to be in Haiti now. His country is in turmoil because Napoleon is sending troops to quell Haiti's attempts to gain independence. The man is King Dick (William Marshall) and, after learning Hamlin's mission, he offers to guide him to the plantation of Gabriel D'Autremont (Charles Corvin), an aristocratic French landowner who is the fiancee of Lydia Bailey and a staunch ally of Napoleon. King Dick is a supporter of Toussaint L'Ouventure (Ken Renard), the leader in the fight for independence.

King Dick and Alboin on a treacherous trek through the jungle

Alboin, Lydia, and her maid Marie

The journey to the plantation is a dangerous one as the jungle is the domain of the outlaw Mirabeau (Roy E. Glenn) and his band of black renegades. Hamlin, disguised as a mulatto field hand, and King Dick eventually arrive at their destination where Hamlin is instantly smitten with the beautiful and haughty Lydia. At first Lydia refuses to sign the document but eventually agrees under the condition that Hamlin takes her maid Marie (Juanita Moore) back to America so she can be reunited with her fiancee.

When Mirabeau and his followers attack the plantation, Hamlin, Lydia, and Marie are forced to flee for their lives disguised as black refugees. The French troops arrive in Haiti led by Napoleon's brother-in-law General Charles Leclerc (Luis Van Rooten) and Toussaint's army of patriots engage them in a bloody battle. When the French occupy Cap Francois, Lydia and Hamlin help foil Leclerc's plan to capture Toussaint. Toussaint and his followers set fire to the city and, as Cap Francois is engulfed in flames, King Dick helps Hamlin, Lydia, and Marie get to the harbor where an American ship will take them to safety.

As was usual for a Fox film, *Lydia Bailey* opened at the Roxy Theatre in New York. The anonymous *New York Times* reviewer said that the facts in both the novel and movie had been "fancifully warped" but found "This period adventure, which merely nods to history on occasion, succeeds in being a briskly paced, swashbuckling yarn." The review goes on to say, "William Marshall makes an imposing and indestructible patriot whose voice is as commanding as his figure. Dale Robertson is dashing as the attorney; Anne Francis is blonde, pretty and as out of place as an iceberg in this setting." *Variety* also found Dale Robertson to be "dashing" and felt that he "neatly meets the demands of the role."

Lydia Bailey had originally been budgeted at $3 million but I suspect this was reduced when the scope of the film was scaled down following Tyrone Power's departure and the decision not to shoot on location. Nevertheless it is still an elaborately mounted production which is often exciting and always visually beautiful. The spectacular fiery climax is particularly impressive. Unfortunately, indifferent audience response to *Lydia Bailey* resulted in a disappointing take of only $1.75 million at the U.S. box office.

I have read in several sources that *Lydia Bailey* was scheduled to be shown on NBC's *Saturday Night at the Movies* in 1963 but it was cancelled because of a subplot involving miscegenation which was deemed inappropriate for television. Since no such subplot is featured in the film, I would conjecture that the cancellation was in response to the volatile state of race relations in the United States at the time, particularly in the South. In January 1963, Governor George Wallace of Alabama had declared in his inaugural speech his intention to protect segregation. In response to this, rumblings of racial unrest were being felt throughout the country. Showing *Lydia Bailey* could actually have been made a positive statement against black oppression but instead NBC took the coward's way out.

The great contribution of *Lydia Bailey* to motion picture history was the movie debut of William Marshall. Marshall studied at New York's Actors Studio and first appeared on Broadway in the original 1947 production of the musical *Carmen Jones*. He acted in many stage productions of Shakespeare and was most noted for his performances as *Othello*. The theatre critic at the *London Sunday Times* called him "the best Othello of our time" and went on to say, "Mr. Marshall rode without faltering the play's enormous rhetoric, and at the end the house rose to him."

In 1953 William Marshall was cast as the lead in a TV series called *Harlem Detective* to be filmed in New York City. The show was cancelled when an anti-Red publication accused him of having Communist connections. Oddly this didn't seem to have affected his film career because he appeared in *Demetrius and the Gladiators* shortly thereafter.

Hollywood never really served William Marshall well. King Dick was probably the best part he was ever given in a film but his most famous movie role was *Blacula* (1972). Made at the height of the blaxploitation craze, Marshall agreed to take the part only if he could have some input into the creation of the character. Thanks to Marshall the "Andrew Brown" character in the original Joan Torres and Raymond Koenig script became "Mamuwalde", an African prince who confronts Dracula in 1780 about stopping African slave trade. Dracula responds by turning Mamuwalde into the vampire Blacula. Reawakened in modern Los Angeles, Blacula preys on members of the black community. Such was Marshall's acting ability that he was able to infuse this seemingly risible premise with credibility and a measure of grace. *Variety* said "William Marshall plays the title role with a flourish." *Chicago Sun Times* critic Roger Ebert said he played the part "with terrifying dignity." The movie proved to be a big hit and Marshall reprised the character in *Scream Blacula Scream* the following year.

William Marshall

Although William Marshall appeared on many television series, including a memorable turn in a 1968 episode of *Star Trek,* his "King of Cartoons" character on *Pee-wee's Playhouse* garnered him the most audience recognition. Blacula and the King of Cartoons brought him a modicum of widespread popular fame but Marshall's most lasting legacy would be as an acting and arts teacher for the African-American communities in Los Angeles and Chicago.

Anne Francis had been "discovered" by Darryl Zanuck when he saw her in the 1950 low-budget film *So Young, So Bad*. He signed her to a seven year contract and her first film at Fox was the 1951 comedy *Elopement* starring Clifton Webb. During the filming of her next movie, *Lydia Bailey,* she was given a big star buildup but suffered anxiety at the thought of being held to a seven year contract at Fox. In October 1952, troubled over the poor box office results of *Lydia Bailey,* the studio let Francis know that they were considering canceling her contract. Zanuck

Anne Francis takes out her frustrations on Dale Robertson in a publicity pose for *Lydia Bailey*

relented and featured her in *Dreamboat* (1952), again with Clifton Webb. In 1953 Fox loaned her out to Warner Bros. for *A Lion in the Streets* starring James Cagney. That same year she did one more picture under her Fox contract; *Rocket Man*, made by Fox's B-picture unit Panoramic Pictures and released in 1954. When Fox terminated her contract in January 1954 Francis said, "In some ways, I'm happy to be out. The free-lance market is pretty good these days." Later that year Anne Francis secured a contract at MGM where she would eventually star in the 1956 science-fiction classic *Forbidden Planet* in the iconic role of "Altaira." Another iconic role for Francis would be private detective *Honey West* in the 1965 ABC television series.

Richard Burton in *The Robe*

10

The Robe
by Lloyd C. Douglas

"I'd marry you if I had to share you with a thousand gods."
– Diana

LLOYD C. DOUGLAS was born Doya Cassel Douglas in 1877 in Columbia City, Indiana. The family later moved to Florence, Kentucky when Douglas' father was assigned as pastor at a Lutheran church there. Doya Douglas attended Wittenberg College in Springfield, Ohio where he studied to enter the ministry. He was ordained as a Lutheran minister at age 26. He later became a Congregationalist and served as a pastor in Indiana, Michigan, Ohio, Washington DC, and Los Angeles. His final ministry was in Montreal, Quebec, Canada after which he gave up the pulpit at age 52. He moved his family back to Los Angeles and decided to write full time under the name of Lloyd C. Douglas. His novels would all deal in some way with religion and philosophy and often feature a doctor as the main character. Douglas had acquired considerable knowledge of the medical profession when he was making pastoral visits to patients at teaching hospitals in the Midwest.

Douglas' first novel was *Magnificent Obsession* which was published in 1929. After the stock market crash, the original publisher, Willet, Clark and Colby, sold the rights to Houghton Mifflin Co. and, through their efforts, *Magnificent Obsession* got on the 1931 best seller lists. The novel was filmed twice by Universal, first in 1935 starring Irene Dunne and Robert Taylor and again in 1954 starring Jane Wyman and Rock Hudson. Both versions were big hits at the box office.

Lloyd C. Douglas had a very successful run of his novels being adapted into motion pictures during the Thirties. Warner Bros. filmed *Green Light* in 1937 starring Errol Flynn and *White Banners* in 1938 starring Claude Raines. In 1939 Paramount made *Disputed Passage* starring Dorothy Lamour. That same year Douglas' novel *Doctor Hudson's Secret Journal* came out. It was a prequel to *Magnificent Obsession* but this book was not made into a movie.

In 1941, Lloyd C. Douglas received a letter from Hazel McCann, a woman from Ohio who was a fan of his novels. In the letter Hazel mentioned that she was curious about what had become of the robe Jesus wore to the crucifixion. Douglas was inspired by this to write his novel *The Robe*, which is "Dedicated with appreciation to Hazel McCann who wondered what became of The Robe." The novel was published by Houghton Mifflin Co. in October 1942 and a month later it reached the No.1 spot on the *New York Times* list of Best Sellers. *The Robe* would hold this position for almost a year and would remain on the list for two years after that. In 1948 a sequel to *The Robe* entitled *The Big Fisherman* was published. In it Douglas writes of the further exploits of the apostle Simon Peter, a character who figures prominently in *The Robe*.

Lloyd C. Douglas final book was *Time to Remember*, which was the first volume of his autobiography. It was published in 1951, the year Douglas died. The second volume, *The Shape of Sunday*, was completed by his daughters and published in 1952.

THE MOVIE

One day in 1941, Richard Halliday, a stage producer and the husband of Mary Martin, was mowing his lawn and mentioned to his neighbor Frank Ross, a film producer, that author Lloyd C. Douglas was writing a novel about the robe that Christ wore to the cross. Frank Ross was intrigued, contacted Douglas, and purchased the screen rights to the as yet uncompleted novel for $100,000. Douglas stipulated to Ross that when the picture was made he didn't want *The Robe* to be "sex and religion mixed in equal parts, played by stained-glass figures in costumes." He hoped that the movie would be "a deep emotional experience that would make audiences feel better and live better lives for having seen it." Ross stayed in close contact with Douglas while he finished the book and the two often met to confer on various aspects of the story. When the novel

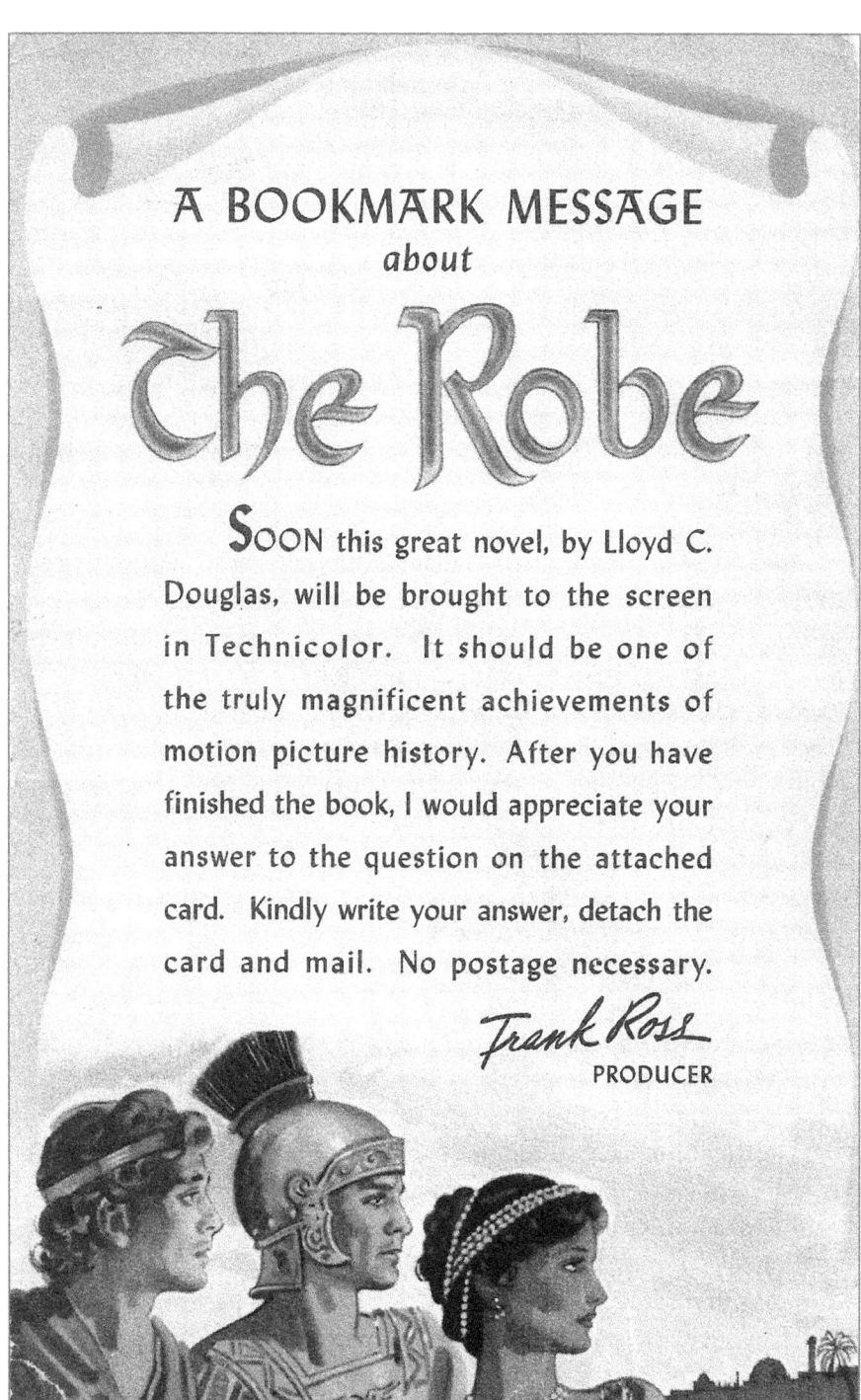

Producer Frank Ross had this "Bookmark Message" inserted into early editions of *The Robe*

was published, Ross had "A Bookmark Message" printed and included in each copy which urged readers to send in a postcard telling him what parts of the story most impressed them.

In 1944, Frank Ross took *The Robe* to RKO who agreed to make the picture in Technicolor with an estimated budget of $4 million. Ross was hoping to begin filming in January 1945 but realized that wartime restrictions would probably delay production. Mervyn LeRoy was lunching with an army chaplain who told him that most of his parishioners had read *The Robe* and "all were eager to see it on the screen." LeRoy went to Frank Ross and told him he would like to direct the film. Ernest Vajda was hired to write the script but Ross and LeRoy were not happy with the results. Vajda was replaced by Albert Maltz, who eventually turned in a massive 277 page screenplay.

One of the earliest pieces to appear in the press about the casting of *The Robe* was a January 3, 1945 article in the *New York Times* stating that Jennifer Jones would portray Diana in the film. Ingrid Bergman had been the first choice but had to withdraw because of other film commitments. In her January 11, 1945 column, Hedda Hopper announced that Allan Dodd, a collegiate wrestler from Tulsa, Oklahoma, had been cast in *The Robe* by Frank Ross and Mervyn LeRoy. Said Hedda, "He's definitely dreamy and strictly swoon stuff." On January 22, 1945, Hedda's rival, Louella Parsons, wrote that production on *The Robe* had been delayed until August 1945 because Mervyn LeRoy had just been contracted by Warner Bros. to direct *The Fountainhead* (it would eventually be filmed in 1949 and directed by King Vidor).

In the July 6, 1945 issue of *The Jewish Post* it was reported that Erich Wolfgang Korngold would be composing the score for *The Robe*. On August 3, 1945, Hedda Hopper ran the following blurb in her column: "Don't be surprised if the role of Demetrius in *The Robe* falls to a newcomer. The dark horse is Tom Holland, formerly of the Merchant Marine. Mervyn LeRoy, who's testing him, has had him in rehearsal for one month in preparation for the event. Holland has received a sharp workout, has had his teeth beautified, and is to be a star entry in a race which has some fancy names mentioned as possibilities, including Gregory Peck." Another newcomer who was put under contract by Mervyn LeRoy for a part in *The Robe* was Quiz Kid Smylla Brind, whose name he changed to Vanessa Brown.

Now Frank Ross was hoping to start production in January 1946, a year after his original date, but again production was delayed. RKO execs criticized the length of the script and Albert Maltz' emphasis on "the mysticism of early Christianity" instead of presenting it as "a way of life." Ross responded by saying he intended to hire Maxwell Anderson and Andrew Solt to revise the script. The April 29, 1948 issue of *Hollywood Reporter* said that Gregory Peck had been signed to play Marcellus Gallio, now under the direction of Victor Fleming. The budget had risen to an estimated $4.5 million. In July 1948 RKO announced that they had cancelled the production because of the high cost involved, although $750,000 had already been spent on the project. Frank Ross argued that the new script Anderson and Solt were working on would reduce the budget considerably and that it could be filmed more inexpensively at the Cinecitta Studios in Rome. The final nail in the coffin of the RKO deal came when the National Catholic Legion of Decency condemned the book and indicated they would ban any film made from it. RKO owner Howard Hughes told Ross that he wanted him to repay the pre-production costs spent by the studio. In January 1950 RKO sued Frank Ross for $1 million and, in April, Ross countersued RKO for $1 million claiming that Howard Hughes had never wanted to make a religious film to begin with. After Lloyd C. Douglas' death in 1951, his estate unsuccessfully attempted to reclaim the movie rights because Ross had not yet produced the film version.

While all this was taking place, screenwriter Albert Maltz came under the scrutiny of the House Un-American Activities Committee. Maltz was subsequently blacklisted and thereafter, when the project was shopped to other studios, Frank Ross would take credit for writing the Maltz screenplay. One of the studios was 20th Century-Fox and, in May 1952, they agreed to purchase the rights to film *The Robe* from RKO. Legal counsel for RKO finally concluded that they could not receive back more than their investment plus interest so Frank Ross and 20th Century-Fox paid the studio $819,000. Zanuck's one reservation about the project was the script Ross presented him. Zanuck was quoted as telling Ross, "I don't like the script at all. You've done it like a cheap piece of melodrama." Thus, in Ross's deal with Fox it was stipulated that the existing script would be rewritten. The script Ross presented was turned over to Gina Kaus who did an adaptation which retained many of the essential themes that Albert Maltz had emphasized. Then Zanuck gave this adaptation to writer Philip Dunne. Typically, Dunne was not anxious to accept the job. In his autobiography he says, "*The Robe,* based on the somewhat simpleminded novel of that name, was an assignment I didn't want which resulted in a screen credit I neither wanted nor deserved." Frank Ross asserted that he had written the original script but didn't want screen credit. Dunne goes on to say, "When no other writer appeared to protest the credit on *The Robe*, I concluded that Frank Ross indeed had written the original script as he claimed and reluctantly allowed my name to appear as sole author of the screenplay." The Albert Maltz writing credit on *The Robe* would not be restored by the Writers Guild until 1997.

In a July 25, 1952 memo to Frank Ross and Philip Dunne, Darryl Zanuck tells them that he has received letters from distributors who complain about too much "talk" in pictures like *David and Bathsheba*. Says Zanuck, "They tell of the disappointment their patrons have experienced on sitting through a picture where there was talk, talk, talk through some of the biggest scenes in the picture." Zanuck did not intend to make the same mistake with *The Robe*.

Frank Ross gave an interview to Louisville, Kentucky newspaper *The Courier-Journal* on September 14, 1952 which said: "Figuratively, it is our aim in producing *The Robe* to reconvert statues and stained-glass figures into human beings whose influence has increased with passing centuries. We hope to follow their hallowed deeds with the camera. We do not want to make the picture a series of spectacles, although a few scenes of pageant proportions are inevitable in a story of an era replete with Roman grandeur. For instance, we have the script boiled down to the best essence of the book, and the budget pared from the RKO minimum of $5,000,000 to a 20th Century-Fox budget of $3,500,000 without sacrificing quality in any respect."

Apparently the script hadn't been "boiled down" enough for Zanuck. On December 19, 1952 he sent a memo to Frank Ross and director Henry Koster saying: " Over the weekend I once again went through the script on *The Robe*. It seems that sometimes we write our scripts to be *read*-rather than to be seen and heard. Although we have now punctuated the script with three or four good violent action sequences, this, nevertheless, is a talking picture. It relies mainly on the spoken word. There is no way to change that entirely but I believe that you boys should once again go through the script page by page, word by word and eliminate any line or speech that may even be halfway superfluous." Consequently Philip Dunne's final draft for *The Robe* runs a comparatively economical 141 pages.

During its long time as an RKO project, a variety of actors, including Gary Cooper, Robert Taylor, and an unlikely Spencer Tracy, had been mentioned for the part of Marcellus Gallio, but when *The Robe* got to Fox,

Darryl Zanuck always intended the role for his favorite star Tyrone Power. Power had appeared in *Mister Roberts* on stage in London for a 23 week run beginning in July 1950. After that he remained in England to star in the film *I'll Never Forget You*, a remake of *Berkley Square*. Zanuck hoped to lure him back to Hollywood by offering him the lead in the studio's most prestigious production. Instead, Power came back to America and opted to star in the play *John Brown's Body*, directed by Charles Laughton. The play toured America prior to opening on Broadway in February 1953, the same month *The Robe* started filming.

With Tyrone Power out of the running, at one point it was considered to make the character of Marcellus older than in the book and approach Laurence Olivier to star. This idea was soon abandoned in favor of casting Richard Burton, who had recently made an impressive Hollywood film debut in Fox's 1952 film *My Cousin Rachel*. Fox had negotiated a three picture loan-out of Burton from British producer Alexander Korda, with the actor getting $50,000 per film. Following *My Cousin Rachel*, Burton appeared in *The Desert Rats* with James Mason as German Field Marshal Rommel. *The Robe* would be the third movie in Burton's three picture deal with Fox. Originally Jean Peters was set to play Diana opposite Burton but she was replaced by Jean Simmons.

Hedda Hopper devoted a large part of her October 1, 1952 column to a casting choice for *The Robe* under the heading "STUDIO SEEKS JEFF CHANDLER FOR KEY ROLE IN *THE ROBE*": "Jeff Chandler has some very enthusiastic fans writing and saying he's the actor to play Demetrius in *The Robe*. They point out that his restrained style of acting is in keeping with the character. I have news on that source. Negotiations are under way to borrow Jeff from Universal-International for the picture. The one factor holding up the deal is that U-I is asking a 20th Century-Fox star in exchange for the loan-out of Jeff. My guess is that the deal will be worked out so that Chandler can do the role. It was a loan-out to 20th for *Broken Arrow* that made Jeff a star."

Jeff Chandler, who badly wanted to play the part, does seem to be inspired casting for Demetrius. Sadly for him, the loan-out never happened and Fox cast Burt Lancaster in the role. Before filming began, Lancaster dropped out and Zanuck looked among his contract stars, finally settling on Victor Mature who turned out to be a perfect choice.

In January 1953 Fox president Spyros Skouras purchased the rights to widescreen movie camera lenses invented in France by Henri Chretien in 1927. Film shot with these lenses would project an image

Richard Burton as Marcellus and Jean Simmons as Diana

two and a half times the width of a normal motion picture. The process was named CinemaScope and it would be the most important innovation in movies since sound. Darryl Zanuck sent a memo to Skoruas which said: "Am absolutely convinced that our big screen French system will have an enormous effect on audiences everywhere and that it is a major development for the industry."

The second week in January the sets for *The Robe* began construction. Over 200 acres of the 360 acre Fox backlot would be devoted to the ten exterior sets for the picture. There would be thirty one interior sets built on the Fox sound stages, including an enormous backdrop of the city of Jerusalem for the crucifixion scene. Shortly after set construction began the decision was made to shoot *The Robe* in CinemaScope and tests were filmed in February 1953 to insure this was feasible. Acting on the side of caution, it was also decided to shoot a standard 35mm version of *The Robe* simultaneously. When the film went into release, only the CinemaScope version would be offered to exhibitors. Because CinemaScope required more intense lighting, a new set-up was required for each version

Victor Mature as Demetrius

being filmed. Jean Simmons later said, "CinemaScope required a lot of extra lights so we were broiling for the entire shoot." Sets were quickly redesigned to accommodate the increased width and director Henry Koster sometimes had to position his actors across them in what Jean Simmons likened to "a police lineup."

Jean Simmons as Diana

Filming began on February 23, 1953 and Richard Burton quickly bonded with co-star Victor Mature. Fox executives had asked that nobody smoke on the set because it "spoiled the image" for a religious themed film. Not only did Burton and Mature smoke but they played craps as well. Burton said of Mature, "I've never known an actor so happily aware of his limitations. He rejoiced in them. He liked to joke that he was no actor and said he had 60 films to prove it. But against him I looked like an amateur." Burton felt he hadn't yet mastered the art of film acting: "Nobody showed me how to do it. I didn't know how to do all the histrionics and make them believable for a wide screen." Jean Simmons concurred: "[Richard Burton] was such an exciting actor. But he was new to films and he wanted to learn how to do it well before the camera, and he didn't have a director who could help him. It all had to be shot so quickly."

Richard Burton thought Jean Simmons was "exquisitely beautiful" and she later confessed that they had a brief affair while making *The Robe*. Jean wasn't Burton's only conquest. Dawn Addams, who plays the small role of Junia in the first scene of the film, said, "I was in my early twenties and still new in films, and Rich swept me off my feet and into bed." I guess smoking wasn't the only thing those Fox execs should have been concerned about.

British actor John Buckmaster joined the cast playing the mad emperor Caligula but this would turn out to be a tragic footnote in the filming of *The Robe*. Buckmaster was born in Essex, England in 1915, the son of actress Gladys Cooper and Herbert Buckmaster. His life would be plagued by mental problems, but his famous mother never came to terms with his illness. From October 1951 to February 1952, John Buckmaster played "The Dauphin" on Broadway in George Bernard Shaw's play *St. Joan*. Shortly before the play finished its run, Buckmaster ran naked out of his New York apartment and attacked a policeman with a knife.

On February 8, 1952 the *New York Times* carried the following news item: "ACTOR SENT TO BELLVUE; Buckmaster is Committed After Knife Threat to Policeman. John Buckmaster, who had appeared recently in the revival of George Bernard Shaw's *St. Joan*, was sent to Bellevue Hospital for psychiatric observation yesterday after he had been arraigned in Felony Court on charges of felonious assault and carrying concealed weapons." Concealed? He was naked!

At some point during the run of *St. Joan*, Fox had taken notice of Buckmaster's performance as "The Dauphin" and a year later he was summoned to the studio to test for the part of Caligula. The casting

Jay Novello (as Tiro the slave merchant), Richard Burton, and Dawn Addams

department was either unaware of or chose to ignore his fragile mental state. He got the part and was fitted for costumes in early March 1953. Shortly after filming began, Buckmaster had a mental breakdown on the set and was taken from the Fox soundstage to a sanitarium. He was in and out of mental institutions for the remainder of his life and committed suicide in 1983.

Prior to the hiring of John Buckmaster another New York based actor, Jay Robinson, had been considered by Fox's casting director William Gordon for the part of Caligula. With Buckmaster abruptly out of the picture, Gordon contacted Robinson's agent to arrange a quick meeting. Gordon interviewed Robinson and then took him to the set to meet with Henry Koster and Frank Ross. Two days later, on March 23, 1953, Delmer Daves directed Jay Robinson's screen test as Caligula. The test was a triumph and Robinson was signed to play Caligula with a two month contract at $3,000 per week. After Robinson completed his first scene on his first day of filming, the crew applauded him. Jean Simmons turned to him and said, "I don't know if you are aware of how rarely that happens." Robinson would later say, "I felt a tremendous affinity for the part." This may have worked well for the picture but it didn't do any good for Jay Robinson's private life, but more on this later.

Jeff Morrow, who made his film debut as the Roman soldier Paulus in *The Robe*, was interviewed by Jim Knusch for the Fall 1993 issue of *Psychotronic Video Magazine*. He had this to say about filming his first movie: "The decision to shoot in CinemaScope happened after the casting and costume fittings. Consequently, to make the necessary changeovers in set design, lighting, and in other technical areas, it caused a delay of

John Buckmaster costume test as Caligula (Courtesy of Photofest)

three weeks. Of course, we all stayed on salary, since actors were paid that way in those years with very few exceptions. The schedule stretched to 10 or 11 weeks of shooting. Being in what was the premier wide screen production generated much excitement in all of us. We were all aware of the fact that *The Robe* would cause a lot of attention for those who were appearing in it"

When I interviewed Fox choreographer Stephen Papich in 2003 he confirmed the excitement felt by everyone at the studio during the production

Jay Robinson as Caligula

Jeff Morrow as Paulus

of *The Robe*. He also told me, "Everybody available on the lot was pressed into service for the crowd scenes. I was one of the Roman slaves at the foot of the cross during the crucifixion scene." Henry Koster even recruited Second Assistant Director Donald Klune to play Jesus. Papich said that Marilyn Monroe wanted to do a cameo but Zanuck rightly felt that her sudden appearance would be disruptive to the movie. In the end he did allow her to dub the slave girl who speaks to Marcellus and Diana on a cliff in Capri: "My lady, a message from the emperor. He'll see Tribune Gallio at once."

On March 25, 1953, Darryl Zanuck issued a memo to Frank Ross and Henry Koster: "Here is further detail on the five reels of rushes I saw last night on *The Robe*. I have great praise for all of the acting and all of the directing. I continue to be concerned about several spots where we appear to be definitely soft or out of focus." The initial use of widescreen was not without its problems, many of which were solved making the second CinemaScope feature, *How to Marry a Millionaire*, which went into production while *The Robe* was still being filmed. The same day Zanuck sent his memo to Ross and Koster he sent another to Nunnally Johnson and Jean Negulesco, producer and director respectively of *How to Marry a Millionaire*: "I see an enormous improvement in the rushes of *How to Marry a Millionaire*. I am not speaking of the acting but of the handling of CinemaScope. In practically every instance of the six reels I ran last night you have perfectly sharp and clear photography with amazing lighting effects. Almost in all instances the composition has been vastly improved over previous material." A less complicated production, *How to Marry a Millionaire* would be finished before *The Robe* but the release was delayed because the studio rightly felt that the latter was a more impressive way to introduce CinemaScope to the public.

The Robe was completed at a cost of $4.5 million dollars, which had been the estimated budget when it was a project at RKO. The New York premiere on September 16, 1953 was, of course, held at The Roxy. During the first week of the New York engagement, *The Robe* set an all time record, more than doubling the normal box office take and making it the most successful attraction at The Roxy up to that time.

The Hollywood premiere was at Grauman's Chinese Theatre on September 24, 1953. Grauman's had the exclusive Southern California engagement of *The Robe* in 1953 and the run was kicked off by a footprint ceremony for Jean Simmons. According to *Boxoffice* Magazine, the Hollywood premiere at Grauman's was one of the most spectacular that Tinseltown had witnessed in years. The Hollywood Chamber of

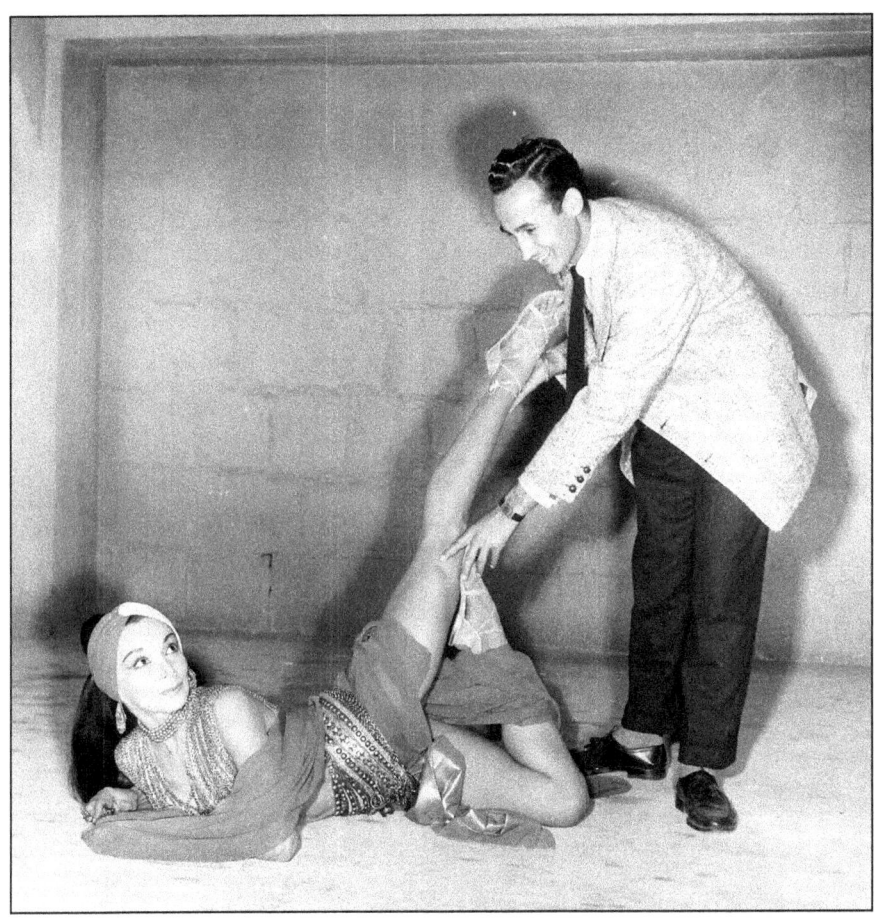

Choreographer Stephen Papich rehearses specialty dancer Virginia Lee on the set of *The Robe*

Commerce renamed Hollywood Boulevard "CinemaScope Lane" and Los Angeles Mayor Norris Poulson proclaimed Thursday "The Robe Day" in the city. 5,000 fans turned out for the event. *The Robe* played at Grauman's for thirteen weeks where it grossed $441,150.

On November 9, 1953, *Time Magazine* reported, "In less than two months, 20th Century-Fox's *The Robe* in CinemaScope has shot to the top of Hollywood's moneymaking list. Playing thus far in only 59 movie houses around the U.S., the $4,500,000 picture has already grossed, says Fox, about $6,5000,000." By the end of 1954 *The Robe* had become the biggest moneymaker since *Gone With the Wind* with a worldwide gross of over $25 million. *The Robe* would hold the position of Fox's highest grossing film until the release of *The Longest Day* in 1962.

Not long before he resigned as Chief of Production at Fox in 1956, a disillusioned Darryl Zanuck complained to Philip Dunne about their recompense for making *The Robe*, "You and I saved the picture but what did we get out of it? Frank Ross walked off with millions in capital gains; we got our salaries and nothing more. Frank deserved it- he had taken the original risk and bullied the project through- but there's something unfair about a system in which a man can make more out of one picture than we can in many years of hard work."

Excerpts from reviews for *The Robe:*

> *New York Times* (September 18, 1953) by Bosley Crowther
> "Twentieth Century-Fox removed the wrappings last night from its much-heralded CinemaScope production of *The Robe* and revealed a historical drama less compelling than the process by which it is shown. An unwavering force of personal drama is missed in the size and length of the show and a full sense of spiritual experience is lost in the physicalness of the display."

> *Time Magazine* (September 29, 1953)
> "*The Robe*", ablaze with Technicolor and alive with romance, action and Biblical pageantry, is Hollywood at its supercolossal best. It also represents an important new technical advance- CinemaScope- that may ultimately doom 3-D as well as ordinary 'flat' movies. Director Henry Koster and Scriptwriter Philip Dunne have made a real effort to avoid the pitfalls of Biblical movies by balancing the saintly preaching of Dean Jagger and Michael Rennie with the muscular Christianity of Richard Burton and Victor Mature. Obviously, Hollywood has finally found something louder, more colorful and breathtakingly bigger than anything likely to be seen on a home TV screen for years to come."

> *Variety*
> "[*The Robe*] is a big picture in every sense of the word. One magnificent scene after another, under the new anamorphic CinemaScope technique, unveils the

splendor that was Rome and the turbulence that was Jerusalem at the time of Christ on Calvary."

Photoplay
"The long-awaited Technicolor version of Lloyd C. Douglas' famous novel is a movie milestone."

Harrison's Reports (September 19, 1953)
"Excellent! Even if it had been produced in the conventional 2-D form, Lloyd C. Douglas' powerful novel of the birth of Christianity in the days of ancient Rome would have made a great picture but, having been produced in the revolutionary CinemaScope process, it emerges as not only a superior dramatic achievement but also as a spectacle that will electrify audiences with its overpowering scope and magnitude."

Look Magazine (September 8, 1953)
"Filmed with power and pageantry for new, huge-screen CinemaScope, the nonstop best seller may be the year's outstanding movie."

The Robe was the recipient of the National Screen Council's 45th Blue Ribbon Award. The council was composed of motion pictures editors of newspapers and magazines, radio commentators, and motion picture chairmen of civic and social organizations. *The Robe* was praised by them as "a great picture in a great new medium."

The Robe was nominated for five Academy Awards including Best Picture, Richard Burton for Best Actor, and Best Color Cinematography. It won for Color Costume Design and Color Art Direction. 20th Century-Fox was given a special Academy Award for the introduction of "the revolutionary process known as CinemaScope." Victor Mature would almost certainly have been nominated for Best Supporting Actor had Zanuck not insisted to the Academy that he was a "star" and not a supporting player. But the most glaring omission in the Academy's list of nominations for *The Robe* was Alfred Newman's brilliant background score, which was one of his finest. Fellow film composer Franz Waxman was so incensed by this exclusion that he resigned from the Academy.

THE ROBE

Released: September 1953. Running time: 135 minutes
In CinemaScope and Technicolor
Produced by Frank Ross
Directed by Henry Koster
Screenplay by Philip Dunne and Albert Maltz
Music by Alfred Newman
Cinematography by Leon Shamroy
Edited by Barbara McLean
Cast: Richard Burton, Jean Simmons, Victor Mature, Michael Rennie, Jay Robinson, Dean Jagger, Torin Thatcher, Richard Boone, Betta St. John, Jeff Morrow, Ernest Thesiger

During the reign of the emperor Tiberius (Ernest Thesiger), the young and irresponsible Roman Tribune Marcellus Gallio (Richard Burton) offends Caligula (Jay Robinson), the heir to the throne. At a slave market Marcellus deliberately outbids Caligula for a Greek slave named Demetrius (Victor Mature). Caligula gets his revenge by having the Tribune sent to the troublesome Roman province of Jerusalem forcing

Demetrius up for auction in the Roman slave market

Marcellus to leave behind the woman he loves, Diana (Jean Simmons). In Jerusalem, Marcellus continues his irresponsible ways while his body servant Demetrius has become curious about a holy man named Jesus. At Diana's intervention, Tiberius recalls Marcellus. Before he can return home, Pontius Pilate (Richard Boone), the Roman governor of Judaea, commands Marcellus to carry out the crucifixion of the supposed religious fanatic Jesus.

Richard Boone as Pontius Pilate

Marcellus and Peter

Caligula condemns Marcellus and Diana to death

The Roman soldiers gamble for Jesus' robe at the foot of the cross and Marcellus wins it. Afterward, Demetrius takes The Robe and runs away.

Marcellus believes The Robe has bewitched him and, on the ship taking him back to Italy, he is haunted by nightmares of the crucifixion which cause him to lose his grip on sanity. Tiberius summons Marcellus to his palace on Capri where he is reunited with Diana. Tiberius instructs Marcellus to return to Judaea to find The Robe and make note of the followers of Jesus. Back in Judaea, Marcellus poses as a Roman merchant buying homespun cloth. At the village of Cana, Marcellus is welcomed warmly by Justus (Dean Jagger), a Christian, and it is through him and some of the other villagers that Marcellus begins to learn about the teachings of Jesus. When the apostle Peter (Michael Rennie) arrives at Cana, he is accompanied by Demetrius, who still has The Robe in his possession. A platoon of Roman soldiers arrives to root out Christians and Marcellus fights against them to defend the village. Marcellus pledges himself to Christ and goes off with Peter and Demetrius to spread the Word of God.

A year later, back in Rome, Caligula is now emperor. He tells Diana that Marcellus has returned to Rome and he wants him arrested. Demetrius has been taken prisoner by the Romans and is nearly tortured to death before Marcellus and a band of Christians can rescue him. During an attempt to take Demetrius to safety, Marcellus is captured by soldiers and put on trial before Caligula. Refusing to deny his Christian beliefs, Marcellus is condemned to death. Diana chooses to join him rather than live under the corrupt rule of Caligula.

While *The Robe* was still in production, Darryl Zanuck anticipated that it was going to be a huge success…and a huge success demands a sequel. Lloyd C. Douglas had written a sequel, *The Big Fisherman,* which continued the story of Peter the apostle. Douglas had been so unhappy with the continual delays of the production of *The Robe* at RKO that he declared he would not allow *The Big Fisherman* to be made into a movie. Undaunted, Zanuck approached Philip Dunne with the idea of an original screenplay using characters from *The Robe*. Dunne thought it was "a hairbrained venture" but he got together with producer Frank Ross and director Delmer Daves and the three of them brainstormed a story. Dunne would write a screenplay, which he considered "a corny exercise in adventure and romance," that continued the story of Demetrius, the character played by Victor Mature in the original film.

Victor Mature as Demetrius

On April 6, 1953, Hedda Hopper announced that Victor Mature and Susan Hayward would star in *The Story of Demetrius,* a sequel to *The Robe.* Philip Dunne finished his script and it was submitted to the Production Code Administration in May 1953. The PCA complained about the violence in the gladiatorial combat scenes and the sexual aspects of Demetrius' seduction away from Christianity. The script was revised and PCA approval was given, although there were still some concerns about the violence. On May 26 it was reported in the trades that Jay Robinson would be reprising his role as Caligula in *The Story of Demetrius* and on May 28, the casting of the principal players was completed when Frank Ross chose Debra Paget to play the Christian girl Lucia.

Filming on *The Story of Demetrius* began three weeks after the end of filming on *The Robe*.

Debra Paget and Victor Mature

A week into filming, the title was changed to *The Gladiators*. Although Fox publicity claimed the new production was budgeted at $3.5 million, in reality it was closer to $2 million. Zanuck charged much of the overage incurred by *The Robe* to *Demetrius*, which may account for the studio's inflated report of the budget. The main expenditure in the production of *Demetrius* was the construction of Caligula's private arena. The rest of the sets were refurbished from *The Robe*.

In August 1953 one of the last scenes to be shot was the assassination of Caligula; the mad emperor felled by a spear thrown by one of the Praetorian Guard. Jay Robinson was prepared to do the potentially dangerous stunt himself but Victor Mature, who never did any stunt, dangerous or not, said, "Are you crazy, Jay? Don't let them throw that thing at you. If the wire breaks you could be blinded or killed. Use a double!" He did not heed Mature's advice and, according to Robinson, the spear slammed into his chest with "explosive force." Eight more takes finally got it right and Robinson spent that evening soaking in a hot tub to recover.

On August 13 the title of the film was changed again, the final choice being *Demetrius and the Gladiators*. Some retakes were made and filming concluded in September 1953, the month *The Robe* went into release. *Demetrius and the Gladiators* would not be released until June 16, 1954.

Prior to the release, Jay Robinson did a 17 state cross-country publicity tour to promote *Demetrius*. As standard for an important Fox picture, *Demetrius* opened at The Roxy in New York and Grauman's Chinese in Hollywood. It played a very successful six weeks at Grauman's.

In the *New York Times*, Bosley Crowther gave *Demetrius* a snarky review in which he seems unaware that *The Robe* made a tremendous amount of money. He wrote, "We've got to hand it to Producer Frank Ross and Philip Dunne, the writer who put this one together out the the whole cloth instead of *The Robe*. They obviously figured that religion may get the people to church, but it takes something more in the way of action to get them into the theatre." Bosley focuses his ire on Jay Robinson: "Every so often, Jay Robinson, who didn't quite split his lungs playing the role of Caligula, the mad emperor of *The Robe*, makes a heroic effort to complete the job in the same role. If we never again see Mr. Robinson, we'll be neither sorry nor surprised." Nasty, Bosley, very nasty. It continues to amaze me that this man, who doesn't seem to like movies or actors, became a film critic.

Variety found both the screen story and Delmer Daves' direction to be "compelling." Their critic praised the cast: "With [Victor] Mature

Gladiators fight to the death in *Demetrius and the Gladiators*

easily winning top acting honors for his splendidly projected Demetrius, he is pressed by Susan Hayward as the evil Messalina, and Jay Robinson, repeating his mad, effeminate Caligula." *Motion Picture* magazine said, "The millions who enjoyed the spectacular movie *The Robe*, have a chance to continue their pleasure at the truly exciting and worthy sequel." *Boxoffice* called *Demetrius* "as shrewd a bit of showmanship as the industry has witnessed in many a year" citing that the movie would appeal to some audiences for its religious aspect. Other theatergoers "who are more materialistic and earthy in their film tastes" would enjoy the "sizable quantities of sex, heroics, and unmitigated ferocity." *Boxoffice* also praised Susan Hayward for giving a "superb performance in an unusually difficult role."

Audiences responded enthusiastically and *Demetrius and the Gladiators* went on to make over $8 million during its initial run. *The Robe* and *Demetrius* were reissued together in 1959 and *The Robe* solo again in 1963.

In 1966 producer Frank Ross sued 20th Century-Fox for $100,000 because Fox had included *Demetrius and the Gladiators* in the original package of films for the first season of NBC Saturday Night at the Movies back in 1961. Ross felt that the studio had "reduced the profits" of the film by selling it as part of a package rather than an individual sale.

DEMETRIUS AND THE GLADIATORS

Released: June 1954. Running time: 101 minutes
In CinemaScope and Technicolor
Produced by Frank Ross
Directed by Delmer Daves
Screenplay by Philip Dunne
Music by Franz Waxman
Cinematography by Milton Krasner
Edited by Dorothy Spencer
Cast: Victor Mature, Susan Hayward, Michael Rennie, Jay Robinson, Debra Paget, William Marshall, Barry Jones, Ernest Borgnine, Richard Egan, Anne Bancroft

Following the death of Marcellus and Diana, Peter (Michael Rennie) leaves The Robe in the care of Demetrius (Victor Mature) and goes off to spread the Gospel. Caligula (Jay Robinson) has now decided that The Robe must possess powers that can raise the dead and commands his soldiers to search the Christian sector of Rome for it. Attempting to defend a Christian girl, Lucia (Debra Paget), from a Roman soldier, Demetrius fights him and is arrested. He is sentenced to be trained as a gladiator in the gladiatorial school of the emperor's uncle, Claudius (Barry Jones).

At the school he is noticed by Claudius' beautiful but dissolute wife, Messalina (Susan Hayward). On his first day in the area, Demetrius defeats his opponent but refuses to kill him. As punishment, Caligula sets loose his

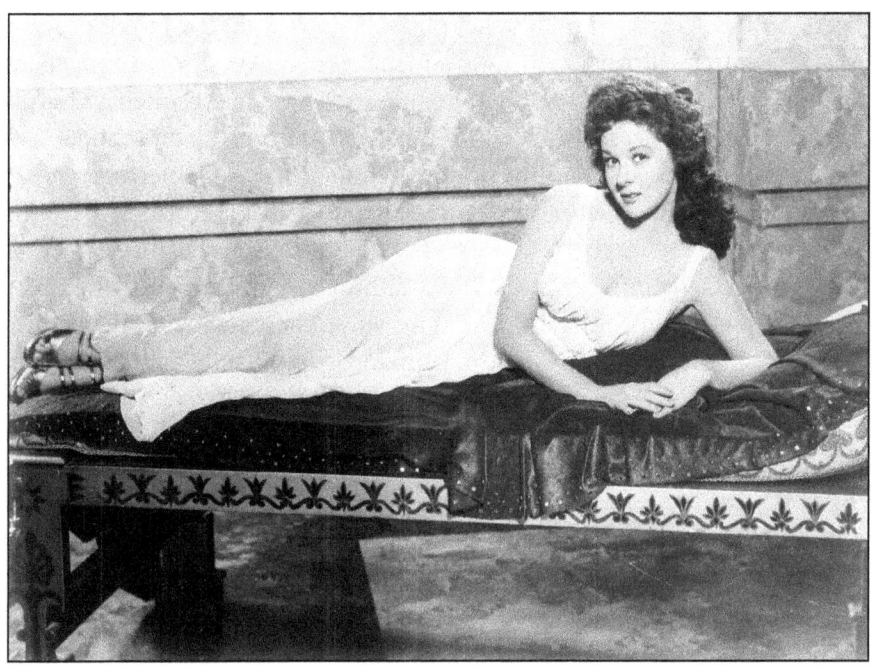

Susan Hayward as Messalina

The gladiator Dardanius attempts to rape Lucia

tigers on Demetrius, who kills them but is badly wounded in the process. Messalina nurses him back to health and makes him her personal bodyguard after he recovers. When Messalina attempts to seduce him, Demetrius rejects her amorous advances and she sends him back to the gladiator school.

When Lucia gains entry to the school to see Demetrius and is assaulted by the gladiator Dardanius (Richard Egan), Demetrius vows to kill him in the arena. The next day Demetrius makes a spectacular showing in Caligula's private arena, killing Dardanius and all the other gladiators set against him. To reward his valor, Caligula makes Demetrius a Tribune in the Praetorian Guard. Convinced of the folly of his Christian beliefs, Demetrius now falls easy prey to Messalina's seductive wiles. Caligula sends his new Tribune in search of The Robe. Demetrius goes among the Christians and discovers that Lucia is in a coma and did not die of her assault as he had believed. He prays to God for her recovery and when she miraculously awakens, Demetrius' faith is restored.

Demetrius takes The Robe to Caligula who has a prisoner killed and attempts to use The Robe to bring him back to life. He fails and when Demetrius learns of this sacrilege he attacks Caligula. For this offense he

Demetrius gives The Robe to Caligula

Demetrius and his friend Glycon (William Marshall)

is sentenced to be executed in the arena but instead the Praetorian Guard turns on Caligula and kills him. Claudius becomes emperor and promises not to persecute the Christians if they give him no reason to do so. The Robe is returned to Demetrius and, as he leaves the palace to return to his people, Messalina looks longingly after him.

Jay Robinson was a New York stage actor who was cast in his film debut as Caligula in *The Robe* at the age of 22. He took to the part with gusto and, by his own admission, felt "tremendous affinity" for the role. So much affinity that he actually began to act like the Roman emperor off set. Jeff Morrow recalled that, while they were making *The Robe,* Robinson, in full costume as Caligula, went to the Fox commissary for lunch. A studio executive was sitting at his favorite table and Robinson ordered him to leave, which he did. Who argues with Caligula?

Fox was so impressed by Robinson's performance as Caligula that he was signed to a contract. At various times he was mentioned to play Napoleon in *Desiree* and Akhenaton in *The Egyptian*.

Caligula (Jay Robinson) strangles Messalina (Susan Hayward)

His next role, however, would be a relatively minor one in *The Virgin Queen* starring Bette Davis as Queen Elizabeth I. Disappointed with the parts Fox offered him (or didn't), Robinson asked to be released from his contract in August 1955. In his autobiography Robinson says "I began changing agents as often as my shirt." Despite this, few offers were forthcoming and the actor turned to drugs. He was a frequent guest at Bel Air pot parties and a raid on his house by the Los Angeles Police Narcotics Squad landed him in jail for drug possession. For the next few years Robinson was in and out of prison on drug related charges.

During this time the only one of his Hollywood acquaintances who kept in contact with him was Bette Davis, with whom he had become friendly while making *The Virgin Queen*. In 1970 Davis even got him a part in her film *Bunny O'Hare*. Robinson later underwent a "spiritual rebirth" and the remainder of his life was, according to his autobiography *The Comeback,* a productive and happy one.

In March 1971, Bette Davis was the subject of the TV program *This Is Your Life*. On it Jay Robinson spoke a heartfelt tribute to Davis thanking her for the moral support she gave him during his years of trouble. Davis had appeared in two films with Robinson, one of them only the year before, and she would later pen the Foreword to his autobiography. But in Robert Wagner's autobiography *Pieces from My Heart*, the actor claims that after the show Davis told Wagner that she didn't know who the hell Jay Robinson was. Really? Why is it that movie star autobiographies often sacrifice truth in favor of a potentially amusing anecdote?

As previously mentioned, *The Big Fisherman* was Lloyd C. Douglas' official sequel to *The Robe*. Producer Rowland V. Lee had met Douglas in 1942 shortly after he completed *The Robe*.

Howard Keel as Peter and Susan Kohner as Princess Fara in *The Big Fisherman*

The author told Lee that his next book would continue the story and be titled *The Big Fisherman*. Lee attempted to buy the screen rights to the book many times during Douglas' lifetime but was always turned down. After Douglas' died in 1951, Lee began negotiations with the Douglas estate, which resulted in a lengthy legal entanglement which lasted for years. Eventually he secured the rights to make *The Big Fisherman*. The multi-million dollar screen version was filmed in 1958 and released as a major roadshow attraction in August 1959. The film turned out to be a critical and financial failure. An independent production, it was distributed by Walt Disney's Buena Vista Pictures, which owns the rights. Other than a heavily edited version which has shown a handful of times on television, the Disney company has never made *The Big Fisherman* commercially available, although recently it was remastered for their archives.

11

The Egyptian
by Mike Waltart

"Revenge leaves you as empty as fame and fortune. Eat your fill of all of them and you're still just as hungry."
— Sinuhe

MIKA WALTARI was a prolific Finnish writer whose output included novels, plays, poetry, and critical journalism. Although he became well known in Scandinavia when he published his first novel *Escaping from God* in 1925, his international success did not come until the publication of his novel *The Egyptian* twenty years later.

Born in Helsinki in 1908, Waltari was the son of a Lutheran minister and was expected to follow in his father's footsteps. After studying for the ministry at the University of Helsinki, Waltari decided that the life of a clergyman was not the right path for him. At age 19 he went to Paris where he wrote his second novel, *My Grand Illusion*. He returned to the University of Helsinki where he majored in literature and philosophy, graduating in 1929. He became a member of "The Torch Bearers", a group of young literary radicals and worked as a journalist traveling throughout Europe during the Thirties and Forties.

In 1938, Waltari's play *Akhnaton* was produced. During the course of doing research for this play, Waltari became fascinated with the subject and began to plan writing the novel which would eventually become *The Egyptian*. World War II put the project on hold and during this time he wrote political propaganda for the Finnish government. *The Egyptian* was eventually finished and published in 1945. The novel was an instant

Edmund Purdom and Bella Darvi in *The Egyptian*

sensation in Finland and soon become a best seller throughout Europe. In 1949 the U.S. rights to the novel were bought by G.P. Putnam's Sons and it was translated into English by Naomi Walford. *The Egyptian* outsold every other novel that year, topping the best seller lists in 1949. It would hold the position of the all-time best selling foreign novel in the U.S. until the publication of *The Name of the Rose* in 1980.

Despite his fame, Waltari remained very private in his personal life. He married Marjatta Luukkonen in 1931 and they remained together until his death in 1979. The couple had one daughter, Satu, who also became a writer. Mika Waltari endures as the most revered and honored writer in Finnish history.

Mika Waltari wrote seven more novels after *The Egyptian*, six of which were historical fiction in a similar vein: *The Adventurer* (1948) and its sequel *The Wanderer* (1949), *The Dark Angel* (1952), *The Etruscan* (1955), *The Secret of the Kingdom* (1959), and *The Roman* (1964). All of these novels were popular but they never achieved the tremendous success of *The Egyptian*. None of them were made into films, although *The Dark Angel,* which takes place during the fall of Constantinople, was optioned by producer Dino De Laurentiis. In 1962 Hugo Butler was hired to do the screenplay which Richard Fleischer would be directing. When Butler became too ill to continue, Dalton Trumbo replaced him as the screenwriter. In February 1963 Trumbo sent his finished script to De Laurentiis and, although the producer was pleased with the results, the project was soon abandoned. Perhaps the unimpressive box office returns on the $10 million dollar De Laurenttis/Fleischer film *Barabbas* (1961) made the producer have second thoughts about making another expensive epic.

THE MOVIE

Although it has been widely assumed that Darryl Zanuck bought the film rights to *The Egyptian* specifically as a CinemaScope follow up to *The Robe,* this is not true. On October 5, 1952 Louella Parsons reported that Zanuck had already secured the rights to the novel with the intention of casting Marlon Brando in the title role. This was only a few months after Fox had obtained the rights to make *The Robe* and before that film had actually gone into production.

The job of turning Mika Waltari's lengthy novel into a screenplay was given to Casey Robinson, a writer who was responsible for penning the scripts for some of Bette Davis' best films at Warner Bros. He had recently written the screenplay for the successful Fox film *The Snows of Kilimanjaro*. His scripts for *The Egyptian* were not so successful. His Revised Temporary script of April 1953 was criticized by both Zanuck and director Michael Curtiz for the language being too "flowery". When he submitted his Second Revised Temporary script of June 1953, Zanuck told him to tone down some of the racier dialogue in scenes involving the courtesan Nefer.

Victor Mature as Horemheb

but Douglas chose to leave the picture altogether. On July 15, 1953 the following appeared in Hedda Hopper's column: "After watching Jay Robinson's work on sound stages, we figured 20th Century-Fox had itself a discovery. So it's not surprising that the studio signed him to a long term contract and cut out a schedule that would keep him hopping. He'll play the young Pharoah in *The Egyptian;* John Wilkes Booth in *Prince of Players;* and likely Napoleon in the film version of *Desiree*. Jay's role as Caligula in *The Robe* and *The Gladiator* did the trick." In November 1953 Hedda was still insisting that Robinson would play the part

Michael Wilding as Akhnaton and Anitra Stevens as Nefertiti

of Pharoah, should Douglas be moved to the leading role, although at this point Robinson hadn't even been tested. In early February 1954 Philip Dunne and Victor Mature pitched Cameron Mitchell to Zanuck who gave the okay to test him for the part of Akhnaton. A month later, Fox finally got around to testing Jay Robinson for the role. John Lund, Hugh O'Brian, and Michael Pate also tested for the part in March 1954. In total, twenty actors did screen tests for the role of Akhnaton before Zanuck decided to borrow Michael Wilding from MGM for the part.

Screen tests for other roles were given to a former Miss Malaya named Violet Sleigh, Fox contract player Virginia Leith, Robert Lippert's girlfriend Margia Dean, cowboy star Guy Madison, Charlotte Austin, and Joan Winfield. Charlotte Austin did appear in publicity shots for the film, dressed in an Egyptian costume and posing with a leopard. Joan Winfield, who was the daughter-in-law of Michael Curtiz, was the only one who ended up with a part in the movie. She played the small role of governess to Pharoah's children.

Another bit of "Curtiz Casting" occurred with Anitra Stevens, who plays Queen Nefertiti in the film. Although studio publicity claimed she had been chosen by Curtiz after he interviewed 67 actresses for the part, Anitra had already appeared in two previous films directed by Curtiz, *The Jazz Singer* (1952) and *Trouble Along the Way* (1953). Years later it was revealed that she was his mistress during this period and beyond. Zanuck had asked screenwriter Philip Dunne to watch over the production and keep an eye on Curtiz in particular. One day an agent brought Dana Wynter into Dunne's office and Dunne felt she would be perfect for the part of Nefertiti. He sent her up to Zanuck's office but on the way she was waylaid by Michael Curtiz who told her the part had already been cast. Anitra Stevens later claimed that she made enough money playing Nefertiti in *The Egyptian* to enable her to buy a house in North Hollywood. Hmmm...

Bella Darvi. Has there ever been a more unjustly maligned actress in the history Hollywood? Born Bejla Wegier in Sosnowiec, Poland in 1928, at the age of twelve she moved with her Jewish family to Paris to escape the Nazis. In a 1954 interview with columnist Sidney Skolsky she said, "When I was fifteen, the Storm Troopers came one night and took us to a concentration camp as Polish aliens." Bejla was released three

Bella Darvi and Michael Curtiz

years later but one of her brothers died there. After the war she married a rich European businessman but they soon divorced. In June 1951, Darryl Zanuck and his wife Virginia were visiting Paris where they were introduced to Bejla Wegier at a sidewalk cafe. Virginia liked her right away and apparently so did Darryl, who began an affair with her almost immediately. Wegier was a gambling addict in debt to the tune of two thousand dollars. Zanuck paid the debt and suggested she visit him and his wife in California. In November 1952 Wegier took up Zanuck's offer and came to Hollywood. The Zanuck's installed her in their Santa Monica beach house, which she shared with their youngest daughter Susan. Susan loathed her on sight. Zanuck decided to give her a screen test and changed her name to Bella Darvi ("Dar" from Darryl and "vi" from Virginia). The test was a success and Darvi was starred opposite Richard Widmark in the CinemaScope film *Hell and High Water*. It was on the strength of this that Zanuck made the decision to cast her as Nefer in *The Egyptian* when it became impossible for him to secure Ava Gardner for the role.

Although Zanuck had always intended for Marlon Brando to play the lead in *The Egyptian*, it was difficult to get the mercurial actor to accept the part. On March 27, 1953, Hedda Hopper said, "Altho he has been reported to be thru with pictures, [Brando] did some hemming and hawing when asked whether he would do *The Egyptian* for 20th." Despite Zanuck's overtures, Brando went to Paris for an extended stay in April 1953. In December Brando was back in New York but still reluctant to commit to *The Egyptian*. Hedda Hopper reported, "I hear Marlon Brando is giving Darryl Zanuck a big headache over *The Egyptian*. He is being difficult. I don't understand why our producers waste so much time on him. We have much better actors than Mr. Brando right here in Hollywood." Zanuck's offer of a $100,000 paycheck eventually changed Brando's mind about playing the part.

By early January 1954 the final version of the script was finished, the parts were cast, sets were being constructed, and costumes were being made. The cast, along with Michael Curtiz and Philip Dunne, assembled for a reading of the script. At this time the cast included Marlon Brando as Sinuhe, Kirk Douglas as Akhnaton, Victor Mature as Horemheb, Gene Tierney as Baketamon, Jean Simmons as Merit, Peter Ustinov as Kaptah, and Bella Darvi as Nefer. Philip Dunne, in an interview for Patrick McGilligan's book *Backstory: Interviews with Screenwriters of Hollywood's Golden Age*, says "'Brando was driven off the picture by Michael Curtiz." According to Dunne, Brando read the part of Sinuhe "absolutely beautifully…It was quite poetic." Curtiz response to his reading was, "How can I, with all my genius, make you play this man who is one moment hero, the next moment villain." After the reading, Philip Dunne spoke with Zanuck and said "Mike [Curtiz] seemed a little confused about the character, and I think Brando was puzzled." That night Zanuck received a call from Brando's agent informing him that Brando was on a plane for New York because, "He doesn't like Mike Curtiz. He doesn't like the role. And he can't stand Bella Darvi." The official reason for his abrupt departure given at the time was that Brando was ill due to overwork and needed to see his psychiatrist. The psychiatrist later reported to the studio that Brando was "very sick and confused." Walking out of *The Egyptian* also cost Brando the lead in Stanley Kramer's upcoming film *Not as a Stranger*. Kramer was not willing to take a chance on the temperamental star.

The first thought was to move Kirk Douglas from Akhnaton to the part of Sinuhe but then the actor announced that if Marlon Brando was out, so was he. Bye, bye Kirk. Hello more casting problems. Biographer Mel Gussow quotes Zanuck as saying, "It took about four hours but we borrowed Edmund Purdom who was under contract to Metro." It wasn't quite that simple.

The first thing Zanuck did was to slap Brando with a $2 million breach-of-contract lawsuit. This was eventually settled when Brando agreed to play Napoleon in the forthcoming Fox movie *Desiree*. Fox approached English actor Dirk Bogarde to replace Brando. Bogarde was happy to accept the part of Sinuhe but Fox had a clause in his contract which obligated him to make one film a year for the studio over the next five years, whether he liked the projects offered to him or not. In his authorized biography by John Coldstream, Bogarde says he told Zanuck, "I refuse absolutely to commit myself in Hollywood without having the right to manage my own career by being able to say no to a part I don't like." J. Arthur Rank, Bogarde's studio in England, was having none of it either. Dirk Bogarde commemorated this incident by naming one of his dogs Sinhue.

Of course Hedda Hopper had an opinion. In her February 18, 1954 column, Hopper said, "Since Darryl Zanuck is having difficulties in casting the leading role in *The Egyptian*, I'd like to suggest an actor I saw on the *Omnibus* TV show. He played a Mexican bullfighter who knew he was about to die. His name is John Cassavetes." Such was the power of this Hollywood gossip monger that Zanuck took her seriously and brought in Cassavetes from New York for a screen test. Philip Dunne met him and felt he would be better suited to play Akhnaton. He eventually didn't get either part but he did call Hedda Hopper to thank her: "Whether I get the part or not your call has opened up a new life for me. I've been approached about playing Joseph in *Joseph and His Brethern* [it was never made], offered parts in two Broadway plays and four television shows."

In his error riddled 2007 autobiography *Include Me Out*, Farley Granger claims that after he saw Granger's performance in *The Girl in the Red Velvet Swing*, Zanuck offered him the lead in *The Egyptian*. Considering that *The Girl in the Red Velvet Swing* was made the year after *The Egyptian*, this is dubious information to say the least.

Darryl Zanuck was very anxious to get *The Egyptian* into production. Recent archeological discoveries made ancient Egypt a topical news item and other studios were planning their productions set in Egypt. MGM had *Valley of the Kings*, Columbia was starring Rita Hayworth in *Joseph and His Brethren*, Howard Hawks was directing *Land of the Pharaohs* for Warner Bros. and over at Paramount Cecil B. DeMille was working on

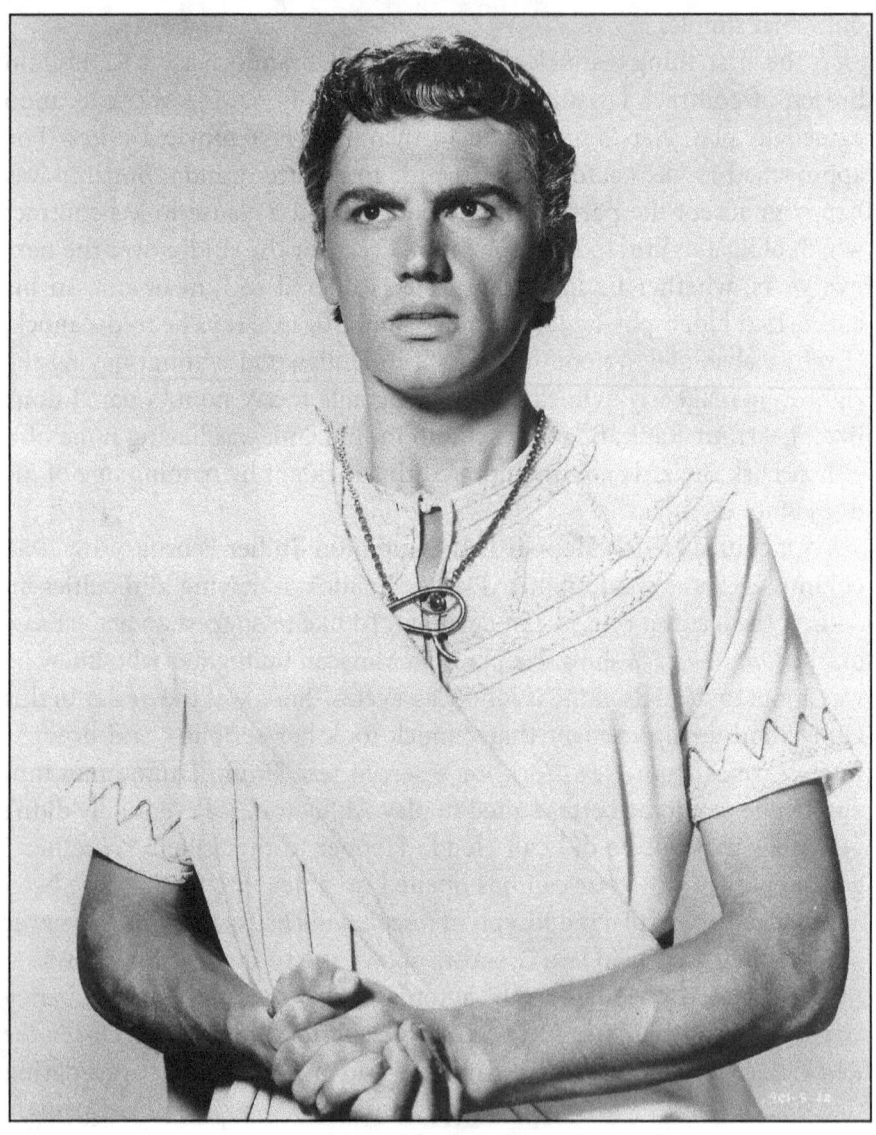

Edmund Purdom as Sinuhe

a little film called *The Ten Commandments*. Zanuck was determined to make *The Egyptian* the most authentic of them all and employed an army of researchers including Elizabeth Riefstahl, the Assistant Curator of Egyptology at the Brooklyn Museum to ensure the accuracy of sets, props, and costumes. All this and still no leading man. Montgomery Clift, John Derek, and Rock Hudson were considered but rejected. Hedda Hopper said that Clift was "dying" to play the part. And then Darryl Zanuck saw Edmund Purdom in *The Student Prince*.

Edmund Purdom was born in 1924 in Hertforshire, England. After serving in the army during World War II, Purdom joined the Royal Shakespeare Theatre at Stratford-upon-Avon. There he was noticed by Laurence Olivier who invited him to join the Olivier/Vivien Leigh company on its U.S. tour. Purdom appeared with Olivier and Leigh in *Caesar and Cleopatra* and *Antony and Cleopatra* on Broadway where he attracted the attention of Hollywood talent scouts. He decided to leave the company and try his hand at Hollywood. Purdom tested at Warners for *Force of Arms* (ironically, the test was directed by Michael Curtiz), Universal for *The Mississippi Gambler,* Fox for *My Cousin Rachel,* and MGM for *Rhapsody*. He didn't get any of the parts but he did get small roles in Fox's *Titanic* (1953) and MGM's *Julius Caesar* (1953) starring Marlon Brando, which lead to his being signed to a contract at MGM. When singer Mario Lanza was fired from *The Student Prince*, Purdom replaced him, lip-syncing to the songs Lanza had already recorded. The movie was a big hit and Purdom was heralded as an important new star. Darryl Zanuck approached MGM about borrowing Edmund Purdom for *The Egyptian* and, knowing Zanuck was in a tight spot, MGM demanded $300,000 for the loan out. Zanuck agreed and, at last, *The Egyptian* was ready to go before the cameras.

Principal photography on *The Egyptian* commenced on March 3, 1954, long after the original proposed start date of December 19, 1953. Cinematographer Leo Tover had already taken a second unit location crew to Egypt to photograph the background footage for the film's prologue and various shots of the Nile which appear throughout the movie. The rest of *The Egyptian* was filmed on the Fox backlot, with the exception of the "lion hunt" sequence which was shot at Red Rock Canyon located two hours north of Los Angeles. As previously mentioned, Zanuck had asked Philip Dunne to keep watch over the production. Dunne later said the Curtiz was "rehearsing the stand-ins instead of the cast, establishing movements which the actors would then have to come in stone cold and duplicate."

Photos taken on the set show a different story, with Michael Curtiz closely conferring with his cast members but, as none of the principal players are alive now, who can say for sure what went on. Peter Ustinov did make his often quoted quip "It was like being in a monstrously huge set for *Aida* and not being able to find the way out." Michael Wilding said "I knew it would be a disaster from the word go, but another child was on the way and I could not allow myself the luxury of being put on suspension again

Gene Tierney (with friend) as Princess Baketamon

for rejecting a role." Why Wilding felt this way is a mystery as he was given far worse assignments at MGM, a prime example being *Torch Song* with Joan Crawford.

Prince Aly Khan was courting Gene Tierney at the time of filming and often appeared on the set to visit her. In her autobiography Tierney, who was playing the role of Princess Baketamon in the film, says "[Aly] remarked one day on the authenticity of the props and special effects. Harry Brand, the publicity head at Fox, quickly sent out a press release saying that Aly Khan was serving as our unpaid 'technical advisor.' He was, in fact, an authority on Egyptian history." Gene Tierney was in an increasingly emotionally fragile state during the filming of *The Egyptian*. Of this she later said, "My role did not seem to be hurt by the fact that I was sinking into a deeper depression. My princess was shrewd, disturbed, unstable, and menacing. I can only believe I played her faithfully." She did most admirably.

On April 15, 1954, Zanuck sent Alfred Newman, the musical director at Fox, a memo stating that "I am now commencing to cut the picture sequence by sequence even though we do not finish photography until sometime in May. The world premiere is set for September 1st." Zanuck goes on the say that although he would like to have Newman score the film he does not believe this is possible because of Newman's commitment to the musical *There's No Business Like Show Business*. Zanuck suggests that either Franz Waxman or Bernard Herrmann should score *The Egyptian*, with a preference for Waxman because he is faster. Newman chose Herrmann to do the score but then Zanuck moved up the release date, leaving only five weeks to compose the music. Bernard Herrmann knew this was an impossible task so he proposed to Alfred Newman that they collaborate. Each of them took certain portions of the story and set to work. They only met twice during the composing process to smooth out any stylistic differences.

In a memo to Michael Curtiz dated April 29, 1954, Zanuck said, "Last night I ran practically all of the cut material and assembled material on *The Egyptian*...I am sure you know we face a very difficult situation. Two rival companies are trying to beat us out with stories in an Egyptian background. Therefore, in this case I have to gamble and disregard protocol and have the picture cut so that we can get it into music shortly after you have finished final photography."

One of the last scenes shot for the film was the impressive procession of Victor Mature as the new Pharaoh entering the throne room. In his

A costly procession...shot twice

autobiography Philip Dunne says, "It took three cameras, four hundred extras, a hundred technicians, and six hours to shoot." Dunne thought it all went beautifully but the next day Michael Curtiz insisted on staging the entire scene all over again. Dunne protested the re-shoot but Curtiz said "I don't want you standing back on me having ideas!", whatever that meant. Later, after viewing the rushes of this scene, Zanuck sent for Dunne and admonished him for having talked "poor Michael Curtiz into shooting a totally unnecessary scene at a cost of thousands of dollars and a full extra day of shooting time." Dunne responded with stunned silence. Zanuck laughed and said "I knew the son of a bitch was lying to me."

Shooting for *The Egyptian* wrapped in early May. The budget had been estimated at $4 million but in the end it had cost close to $5 million. A great amount of money had been spent on screen tests which were reported to have totaled 21,000 feet of film. Even Nefer's cat was expensive. "Tuffy" got $1000 to hiss in the film. Sixty seven sets had been designed and built by Art Directors Lyle Wheeler and George Davis at a cost of $605,000, the most expensive being the throne room which cost $85,000. Thousands of props, costumes, wigs, and pieces of jewelry had been specifically made for the film. Some of the cost for these was recouped when Paramount bought them for DeMille's *The Ten Commandments*.

On May 28, 1954 Hedda Hooper's column said, "We may have another *Gone With The Wind* on our hands. After the big brass at 20th saw completed footage of *The Egyptian*, they felt it would be a pity to lose any of it on the cutting room floor." Two weeks later *Hollywood Reporter* said the film would be shown with an Intermission. Neither of these statements turned out to be true as Zanuck adhered to his edict about the running times of motion pictures and *The Egyptian* was edited to a length of 139 minutes. Nevertheless it appears as if very little was cut from the film. If existing stills are any indication, there are only a small number which show scenes that don't appear in the final cut.

Prior to the release of *The Egyptian*, a June 1954 edition of *Hollywood Reporter* had a blurb saying that Zanuck would be going to Egypt "to inspect the new archeological discoveries at the tomb of Cheops" in preparation for a proposed sequel to *The Egyptian*. On June 9, 1954, Louella Parsons said, "With the permission of the Egyptian government

Cut scene: Sinuhe and Horemheb graduate from the School of Life (Richard Allan is on far left)

Cut scene: Horemheb and Kaptah (Peter Ustinov) find Sinuhe in the Valley of the Kings

assured, Darryl Zanuck takes off Friday for Egypt to film the funeral ships located near Cairo. Two 20th camera crews make the trip with the boss to film the 'Ships of Death' which archaeologists say may be from 2,500 to 5,000 years old."

Darryl Zanuck decreed that the publicity campaign for *The Egyptian* would surpass that of any Fox film in the past. Fox vice-president Charles Einfeld embarked on a six-week trip to Europe to set up the international premiers for the film (*The Egyptian* would have its European premiere on October 14, 1954). The exhibitors magazine *Motion Picture Daily* reported Fox's publicity efforts continually prior to the film's premiere, which was now set for August 24. Beginning July 1, over 267 cites across the nation would be visited by 20th Century-Fox's two mobile truck units which featured exhibits pertaining to *The Egyptian*. One truck toured the Northern section of the country and the other covered the Southern region. By July 21 attendance for these traveling exhibits had reached the half million mark. Reports said that the exhibits were being attended by 20,000 to 25,000 people per day. The 24 sheet poster billboard campaign was the largest in Fox history up to that time. Thirty five hundred billboard posters were placed in 51 key cities, concentrating on large urban centers and surrounding communities. One hundred and one leading newspapers in 64 cities carried full-page advertisements announcing *The Egyptian*. Fifty-four window displays were planned in New York City stores alone, with eight being at Bonwit Teller's 5th Avenue store. Also in New York City, Gimbel's department store featured the sale of jewelry designs inspired by the movie. In the largest use of television advertising yet by Fox, 160 U.S. and Canadian outlets ran trailers for *The Egyptian*. It was Egyptian mania!

The Egyptian had its sold-out gala world premiere at The Roxy Theatre in New York City on August 24, 1954. It was a benefit charity event with proceeds donated to the March of Dimes. Tickets cost up to

Six Sheet poster art for *The Egyptian*

$100 each. The Los Angeles premiere was held at Grauman's Chinese Theatre on September 1. Edmund Purdom did not attend the premiere. There was already gossip that he was having an affair with actress Linda Christian and planned to divorce his wife. Mrs. Purdom attended the premiere with her mother and said that Edmund had stayed home because he was "terribly overworked" and that all the rumors were "a storm in a teacup."

THE EGYPTIAN
Released: August 1954. Running time: 139 minutes
In CinemaScope and Color by DeLuxe
Produced by Darryl F. Zanuck
Directed by Michael Curtiz
Screenplay by Philip Dunne and Casey Robinson
Music by Alfred Newman and Bernard Herrmann
Cinematography by Leon Shamroy
Edited by Barbara Mclean.
Cast: Edmund Purdom, Jean Simmons, Victor Mature, Gene Tierney, Michael Wilding, Peter Ustinov, Bella Darvi, Judith Evelyn, John Carradine, Carl Benton Reid, Henry Daniell

Exiled to a lonely hut on the shores of the Red Sea, an old man, Sinuhe (Edmund Purdom), is writing the story of his life. As an infant he is found in a reed boat on the banks of the Nile by a physician and his wife who adopt him as their son. Later he attends the School of Life where he studies to become a physician. There he meets the brash Horemheb (Victor Mature) who is training to become a soldier. Together they go lion hunting and save the life of a young man when he is about to be attacked by a lion. This young man is the new Pharaoh, Akhnaton (Michael Wilding), and he rewards Sinuhe by making him the court physician and Horemheb by appointing him to the royal army.

To celebrate, Horemheb takes Sinuhe to a party at the house of a Babylonian courtesan named Nefer ("In their foolishness, men give me the name which means beautiful") and Sinuhe becomes instantly infatuated with her. Nefer (Bella Darvi) frankly tells Sinuhe that she is an evil woman but he refuses to heed her warning. Sinuhe's unrequited lust for Nefer drives him to ruin and despair. Too late he discovers the true love of a tavern maid, Merit (Jean Simmons).

Sinuhe writes the story of his life

Sinuhe flees Egypt and travels around the ancient world for several years, establishing himself as a learned physician and acquiring great wealth in the process. He eventually returns home to find Egypt in the midst of a Holy War. Horemheb, now commander of the army, has allied himself with the priests against Akhnaton who has tried to establish the Sun God Aton as the only true god. From a dying Akhnaton, Sinuhe learns the meaning of life that he had been searching for since childhood.

The Egyptian opened with an impressive take at the box office but business soon trailed off in the wake of mixed reviews. *Life Magazine* said the personal drama was "entombed by the film's ponderous pageantry." This is an odd criticism of the movie as the characters are always at the forefront and the pageantry is minimal when compared to other epics of this type. Other reviews ran the gamut from good to bad.

Akhnation makes Sinuhe the court physician

Hedda Hopper – "*The Egyptian* is a gorgeous 5 million dollar spectacle filmed in the most beautiful color I've ever beheld. Darryl Zanuck spent millions on technical perfection, which overshadows the humans. But Michael Wilding, Jean Simmons, and Peter Ustinov seem in perfect tune with the roles they play."

Variety – "*The Egyptian* is a big and important film in every respect. A big cast with good marquee appeal goes though its paces with obvious enjoyment. In the title part, Edmund Purdom etches a strong handsome profile and brings *The Egyptian* to life."

Bosley Crowther (*New York Times*) – "It glistens with archaeological scenery, rumbles deeply with a sense of human woe- and moves at the pace of a death march across the Roxy's CinemaScope screen."

Saturday Review – "Overlong, overtalky, underacted."

Time – "*The Egyptian* has a kind of blurby, big adjective poetry about it. Authenticity is rampant in every scene."

Motion Picture – "Against brilliant settings that re-created ancient Egypt in fascinating detail, Edmund Purdom dominates a big cast with his dignified portrayal and fine appearance."

In the end, *The Egyptian* made $15 million worldwide. The domestic take on *The Robe* had been $17.5 million but *The Egyptian* took in only $4.25 million in the U.S. Fortunately the international box office was good and the movie, although not the success Zanuck hoped for, made a respectable profit for the studio. The movie received one Academy Award Nomination, for Best Color Cinematography.

Sinuhe falls prey to the temptress Nefer

When *The Egyptian* failed to be the box office blockbuster he had hoped for, Zanuck cancelled plans for the sequel which would have followed the reign of Horemheb and Baketamon. Given the characters enmity toward each other at the end of the film, it would have been interesting to see what kind of sequel could have been concocted. In the novel, when Baketamon is forced to marry Horemheb she despises him so much that she comes up with a unique plan of revenge. She goes to the lowliest men in Thebes, the "donkey men and water carriers and gutters of fish" and invites them to

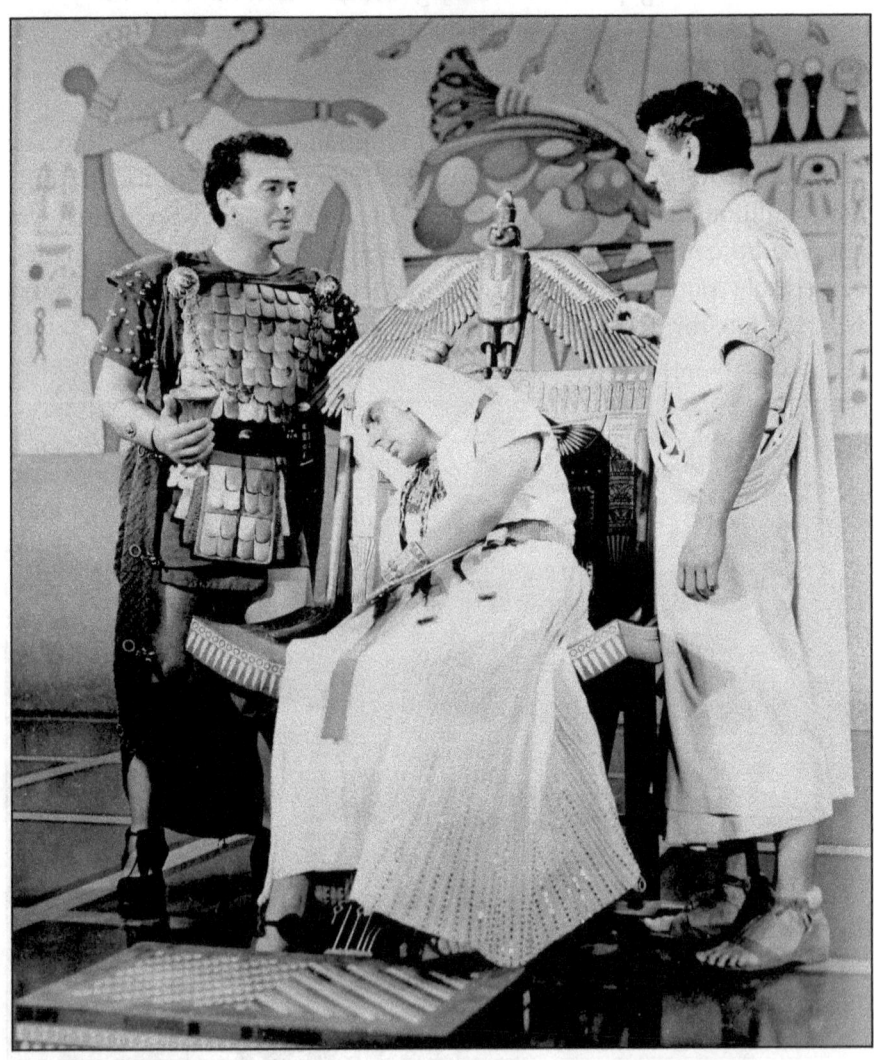

Akhenation dies and Horemheb proclaims himself the next pharaoh

Baketamon and Horemheb

"take their pleasure" with her. As for payment she says, "I desire from each of you no other gift than a stone- and let the stone correspond in size to the pleasure I give you." With these stones Baketamon has a pavilion built in her garden and invites Horemheb to make love to her there. When he arrives she tells him, "Look carefully at these stones. Each one of them- and they are not few- is a memorial of my pleasure in another man's embrace. I have built this pavilion with my own pleasure, and in your honor, Horemheb." You can imagine his reaction. Of course they never would have put anything like this in a movie made in the Fifties. Too bad. It could have been a *Who's Afraid of Virginia Woolf*? set in ancient Egypt.

A curious footnote to *The Egyptian*. On August 30, 1954, six days after the New York premiere of *The Egyptian*, Edmund Purdom had a ceremony in Hollywood to install his foot and hand prints in the forecourt of Grauman's Chinese Theatre. They were quickly removed. Various rumors for the removal of the slab have been given. One says that after *The Egyptian* failed to live up to box office expectations, Fox asked for the slab to be removed. Another claims there was an industry outcry because Purdom had appeared in so few films and he did not deserve the honor. Purdom also incurred the wrath of gossip columnist Louella

Parson when he divorced his wife and took off with Tyrone Power's spouse Linda Christian (Power was a favorite of Parsons). Parsons wrote "I'm on my soapbox about Edmund Purdom" and intimated that he might be a Communist. Purdom made three more films at MGM and all were flops. Nevertheless, he demanded a salary increase. Instead his contract was terminated. Purdom later moved to Europe where he lived and continued to make movies until his death in 2009. The cement slab with his hand and footprints has never been found.

Bella Darvi

Bella Darvi made only one more film for Fox, *The Racers* (1955) with Kirk Douglas. Some of it was filmed on location in Monaco and she decided to return to Europe when it was finished. Prior to this, Virginia Zanuck finally had enough of her husband's paramour and threw Darvi out of the house. Darvi made a few films in Europe and continued to rack up huge gambling debts. Zanuck repeatedly bailed her out of trouble even after he had moved on to other mistresses. In 1968, Darvi unsuccessfully attempted suicide. Once again Zanuck paid her debts but when she had recovered she resumed her obsessive gambling. Zanuck stopped paying her debts in 1970 and in September 1971 Bella Darvi committed suicide in Monte Carlo at the age of 42.

My love of *The Egyptian* goes back a long time and runs very deep. It is the first movie I recall seeing at a theatre, where it was on a double bill with MGM's *Adventures of Quentin Durward*. Afterward I remembered little about *Quentin Durward* but *The Egyptian* was indelibly imprinted on my mind. When the film first appeared on television in October 1962 on NBC Saturday Night At the Movies, I was overjoyed. It was after seeing it again that I read the novel for the first of many times. In those days one was mostly at the mercy of local television programming to see a favorite film. I made a point of catching *The Egyptian* whenever it played, although showings were few and far between. I was always surprised at the poor reputation the film had, not enhanced by the inclusion of the movie in the dreadful Turkey Award books of the Medved Brothers. Those two damaged the reputation of more good movies than I care to think about. Over the years I have shown *The Egyptian* to many of my friends and all of them, without fail, have liked it and wondered why it is basically forgotten.

The most lasting element of *The Egyptian* for film music enthusiasts was the Decca soundtrack record album which was a best seller and never went out of print after its initial release in 1954. According to Bernard Herrmann's biographer "Zanuck was delighted" with the music and Herrmann found the collaboration to be "a pleasure…I'm very fond of that score." So am I. I wore out three copies of the LP.

Marlon Brando and Jean Simmons in *Desiree*

12

Desiree
by Annemarie Selinko

"In the life of every woman there is only one great love."
– Desiree

BORN IN VIENNA, Austria in 1914, Annemarie Selinko lived a life as dramatic as any of the characters in her novels. She attended the University of Vienna as a history major but soon realized she had a talent for journalism. At age 17 she began writing as a journalist and eventually became an Austrian political correspondent based in Germany for the French newspaper *L'Intransigeant*. She wrote her first novel, *I Was an Ugly Girl* in 1937. In 1938, while covering a League of Nations session in Geneva, she met Earling Kristiansen, who worked for the Danish Foreign Office, and they married shortly thereafter.

Thoroughly opposed to Hitler, the couple went to Denmark when it was announced that Nazi Germany had annexed Austria. During the war Selinko and her husband became involved with the Danish underground. Captured and interred by the Nazis, they escaped in 1943 and fled to Sweden where they stayed for the remainder of the war. Selinko worked for the Swedish Red Cross and, while there, she became an interpreter for Folke Bernadotte, Count of Wisborg, who was a direct descendant of Jean-Baptiste Bernadotte and his wife Desiree. This sparked her interest in these historic personages. In April 1945 Annemarie assisted Folke Bernadotte in his negotiations to bring over 30,000 refugees from Nazi concentration camps to Sweden.

After the war her husband Earling was assigned to London as a member of the Danish Foreign Office and Selinko began writing *Desiree* while they lived there. Later Earling's work took them to France and Selinko used that time to research material for her book. She scoured museums and libraries in Paris and Marseilles to obtain historical background and compiled extensive files on every major character involved in the story. After Earling's assignment in France ended they returned to Denmark and settled in Copenhagen where they had a son and Annemarie finished her book. She dedicated *Desiree* to the memory of her sister Liselotte, who had been killed by the Nazis. It was the last book Annemarie Selinko published. She died in Copenhagen in 1986.

Annemarie Selinko wrote four novels, the afore mentioned *I Was an Ugly Girl, Tomorrow Will Be Better* (1941), *My Husband Marries Today* (1943), and *Desiree,* originally published in 1951 and translated into English by Joy Gary in 1953. Of the four, *Desiree* achieved the greatest success, selling over 20 million copies worldwide. Upon its release in the U.S. the *New York Times* called the novel "a fascinating panorama" and it quickly made their best seller list. With its historical setting and feisty heroine the comparisons to *Gone With the Wind* were inevitable as the trailer for the motion picture version was quick to point out: "The most fascinating novel since *Gone With the Wind*" – Boston Post, "The *Gone With the Wind* of the year" – Chicago Tribune, "Rates along with *Gone With the Wind*" – Houston Press.

I first read the novel *Desiree* back in High School, more years ago than I care to remember. When I eventually saw the film I remember thinking how very different it was from the book. I recently re-read *Desiree* in preparation for this book and was surprised at how closely the film follows the novel. Previously I must have been focusing on what was left out as opposed to what was included. To me, it now seems to be a perfect example of Darryl Zanuck's mandate that "you do not leave out any of the outstanding moments of the book". Those outstanding moments are there, which is really saying something as the novel is 495 pages in length. The novel is broken down into four parts:

Part 1- The Daughter of a Silk Merchant of Marseilles
Part 2- Marshall Bernadotte's Lady
Part 3- Our Lady of Peace
Part 4- The Queen of Sweden

Daniel Taradash's screenplay focuses on the human interaction between the main characters, eliminating most of the military machinations. It also eliminates the fourth part of the novel entirely. This is understandable since the movie is basically about the relationship between Desiree and Napoleon and Part 3 ends when he surrenders to the Allies and turns his sword over to her. This is the climactic moment of their story but in the novel her story continues. However, Taradash does paraphrase one line said by another character in Part 4 and incorporates it into Napoleon's final speech in the movie: "How strange, madame, that the two outstanding men of our times have been in love with you. You're no real beauty."

Historians have taken great pains to point out the historical inaccuracies of both the novel and the film. In her "Author's Note" at the end of the novel, Annemarie Selinko says "This book is based on history. In a few incidents I have departed from history because I am persuaded that history is not always recorded to the last detail. In the light of my own interpretation of the characters and of their reactions I, for one, have chosen to believe that what might have happened did happen." Despite whatever liberties may have been taken with the facts, there is still enough historical detail to give the reader more of an understanding of the time, place, and people than would many history books on the same subject.

THE MOVIE

20th Century-Fox was quick to realize the screen potential of *Desiree* and purchased the movie rights in March 1953. In August 1953 Hedda Hopper reported that Julian Blaustein, who would be producing the film version of *Desiree,* wanted Audrey Hepburn for the title role and Marlon Brando for Napoleon. She also said that Blaustein would be going to Europe for two months to scout locations for three films- *Desiree, Hotel Tallyrand,* and *The Racers.* The following month, Louella Parsons noted that Darryl Zanuck had gone to London with the script of *Desiree* to try and convince Vivien Leigh and Laurence Olivier to star in the picture, which Zanuck then planned to film in Europe with Anatole Litvak as director. Vivien Leigh's ill health and Litvak's eventual refusal to shoot *Desiree* in CinemaScope put an end to these plans. In her February 4, 1954 column, Hedda Hopper announced with her characteristic humility that she had predicted eight months ago that Jean Simmons would be starring in *Desiree.* Jean Simmons response was, "I haven't heard about it. How's about reading the book and telling me what kind of part I'll play." Later in February, *Daily Variety* reported that Anatole Litvak was officially off the project because of a dispute "over the process in which *Desiree* should be produced." Noel Coward was briefly considered to replace Litvak, just in case the Oliviers changed their minds, but Henry Koster was the final choice for director.

Although producer Blaustein had already stated his preference for Brando as Napoleon, the part was first offered to Montgomery Clift, who turned it down. Louis Jourdan was also considered for the role. On March 12, 1954 Hedda Hopper stated that Victor Mature had been cast in *Desiree* in the role of Marshall Bernadotte. Later in March, Hopper disclosed that although Fox "is suing Marlon Brando for refusing to do *The Egyptian*, he's still the studio favorite to play young Napoleon in *Desiree*. This role he loves, and if he accepts, 20th will call off its legal eagles in the twinkling of an eye." Fox hit Brando with a $2 million breach-of-contract suit but

Marlon Brando as Napoleon

offered to drop it if he would agree to play Napoleon. Also in March, Jay Robinson, who had made a great impression as Caligula in *The Robe* and *Demetrius and the Gladiators*, was tested for the part of Napoleon but it was thought an established "star" was needed for such an important role. In his 1979 autobiography *Comeback,* Jay Robinson says, "The truth was that Marlon Brando was being truculent in his demands and the studio was using my name to soften his stand."

The cast of *Desiree* continued to be a topic of interest for Hedda Hopper. Her May 14, 1954 column was headlined "Edmund Purdom Fails in Plea to Enact Prince Bernadotte." The paragraph goes on to say that "Edmund Purdom begged to play Prince Bernadotte but the plum part went to Michael Rennie. Jean Simmons' choice was Michael Wilding, but he's busy at Metro."

Despite Hedda Hopper's claim that Brando loved the role, director Henry Koster later stated that it was a difficult film to make because Brando didn't want to play Napoleon and felt it simply "wasn't his part." Koster had done considerable research on Napoleon but knew "Marlon had only made a superficial study of Napoleon." Koster went on to say, "We had some little discussions about how Napoleon should be played, because I had a different opinion on the way it should be acted." Brando's response to Koster was always "I have to play it, and that's the best I can do." On the other hand, Koster loved working with Merle Oberon, whom he felt was "the most beautiful woman."

After several years absence from the screen, Merle Oberon had been cast as Josephine. In a 1982 interview Merle Oberon said of working with Brando, "Believe it or not, we had the most fantastic relationship. He had such respect for me. He was co-operative with me but not with the others. They had a terrible time with him. One of their complaints, and there were hundreds, was that he would mumble his lines in rehearsals, and when the scene came he would scream at them and they wouldn't know how to take it. I found him fantastic." Oberon may have been a bit deluded about the respect Brando had for her as Brando biographers claim that he continually mocked her posh British accent and this made her tense and uncomfortable on the set.

Marlon Brando said of his experience working on the film that he found Henry Koster to be "a kind and pleasant man" but felt he was a "lightweight" director. Although Koster said that there was "endless tension and friction" between them on set, off set Koster and Brando remained friendly and socialized at the director's home on weekends. Brando

Merle Oberon as Josephine and Marlon Brando

was most impressed by Jean Simmons. He thought she was "winning, charming, beautiful and experienced." Of the finished film, Brando found it to be "superficial and dismal". Jean Simmons also expressed no love for *Desiree*, "That's what I call a 'poker-up-the-ass' part. You know, those long-suffering, decorative ladies. I mean, they're very boring." She also recalled being "in complete awe" of Brando, "I was more inclined to watch Marlon playing Napoleon than to attend to my own acting of the scene."

Cameron Mitchell, who played Napoleon's brother Joseph, thought that Brando took advantage of Henry Koster whom Mitchell felt was "A nice man to work for, very pleasant. He never hurt people." Mitchell said, "Marlon didn't give a damn. He was fucking 20th Century-Fox." Mitchell claimed that Brando refused to rehearse. Instead "He would walk onto the set and go from chalk mark to chalk mark without the slightest show of interest. He flubbed and fumbled and fluffed his way through everything."

Prior to principal photography, cinematographer Edward Cronjager and second unit director Fred Fox had taken a crew to France to film backgrounds. The remainder of the movie was shot in Hollywood and

Jean Simmons appears to be contemplating her "poker-up-the-ass" part as Desiree

Monterey, California. Author Annemarie Selinko had been asked to serve as a technical advisor on the film but declined. She did, however, enthusiastically approve of the casting. One member of the cast ended up being a casualty of the editing room. Famed British character actress Cathleen Nesbitt was cast as Napoleon's mother but most of her part was cut from the finished film. Although she is still listed in the film credits and on the posters, she can only be glimpsed briefly during a banquet scene seated at the right hand of Napoleon.

Another casualty of the *Desiree* filming, but in a very different way, was Rita Moreno. In 1954 she had been signed on as a Fox contract player. She met Marlon Brando while visiting the set of *Desiree* and, in her words, "It was lust at first sight. It was a relationship built on sexuality and sensuality." Their on again, off again relationship lasted eight years and when Brando pressured her to have an abortion, Moreno unsuccessfully attempted suicide.

Desiree had its gala world premiere in San Francisco on November 16, 1954. This was a benefit for the San Francisco Newspaper Guild. The next evening the New York opening at the Roxy Theatre was a gala benefit for the March of Dimes. *Desiree* had its Hollywood premiere at Grauman's Chinese Theatre on November 19, where it enjoyed a very successful five week run.

It seemed as if the critics had it in for *Desiree,* and particularly Brando, before the movie even opened. *Time Magazine* had already featured him as Napoleon on the cover of its October 11, 1954 issue with

Can you spot Cathleen Nesbitt in this banquet scene?

the byline "Too Big for His Blue Jeans?" The accompanying profile stated "Nobody, nothing, no amount of money can make him behave." *Variety* began its review of *Desiree* with, "There is a theory in Hollywood that nothing bogs down a historical film as easily as the facts of history. It is a maxim which 20th Century-Fox must have had very much in mind when it CinemaScoped Annemarie Selinko's bestselling novel *Desiree*." Bitter Bosley Crowther was true to form in his November 18, 1954 *New York Times* review. He said, "A great deal of handsome decoration and two talented and attractive stars have been put into the CinemaScope production of the historical romance *Desiree*. The only essential missing is a story of any consequence". Of the cast he said, "Marlon Brando's Napoleon is just a fancy (and sometimes fatuous) facade. The same must be said of Jean Simmons' performance as Desiree. It is pretty but pointless. The others in the cast are mostly robots." Crowley oh so cleverly ends his review with the comment "a streetcar named Desiree." Dilys Powell, writing for the London *Sunday Times* thought Brando "sounded like Ethel Barrymore doing a poor imitation of Noel Coward." One of the positive reviewers was Lillian Blackstone. In her November 27, 1954 *St. Petersburg Times* review "Age of Napoleon Lives Again in *Desiree*" Blackstone found Brando's performance to be remarkable and felt that "he never moves out of character."

In spite of a mostly negative response from film critics, *Desiree* proved to be a popular success with audiences. Filmed at a cost of $2.72 million the movie made $4.5 million in domestic rentals alone and ranked as the 10th highest grossing film of 1954. *Desiree* was nominated for two Academy Awards, for Best Color Set Decoration and Best Color Costume Design. It won neither. Merle Oberon said, "They wanted to give me an Oscar for [Josephine]. There was a big to-do because it was a vignette, it wasn't a big role. They wanted to do this as a supporting role, and the idea of a star getting the award for a supporting role was not done." Although her performance in *Desiree* is certainly worthy of a Supporting Actress nod, her explanation of why this didn't happen is a curious one.

Marlon Brando did win the Best Actor Oscar for 1954…but not for *Desiree*. His other 1954 motion picture, *On the Waterfront,* was a darling of the critics and won the Best Picture award that year. In audience popularity it ranked 15th at the box office, well behind *Desiree*.

DESIREE

Released: November 1954. Running time: 110 minutes
In CinemaScope and Color by DeLuxe
Produced by Julian Blaustein
Directed by Henry Koster
Screenplay by Daniel Taradash
Music by Alex North
Cinematography by Milton Krasner
Edited by William Reynolds
Cast: Marlon Brando, Jean Simmons, Merle Oberon, Michael Rennie, Cameron Mitchell, Elizabeth Sellars, Evelyn Varden, Isobel Elsom, John Hoyt, Richard Deacon

The story begins in Marseilles in 1794 when Desiree Clary (Jean Simmons), the daughter of a wealthy silk merchant, befriends Joseph Bonaparte (Cameron Mitchell) and his brother, a down on his luck general named Napoleon (Marlon Brando). Desiree's sister Julie (Elizabeth Sellars) and Joseph marry and Desiree becomes engaged to Napoleon. After not hearing from him for several months, Desiree learns that Napoleon has been keeping company with the beautiful and aristocratic Josephine (Merle Oberon) in Paris. She goes to Paris and, at the salon of Madame Tallien (Carolyn Jones), finds Napoleon and Josephine together. She throws a glass of champagne at Josephine and reminds Napoleon that she loves him. Desiree contemplates throwing herself into the Seine but is prevented from doing this by General Jean-Baptiste Bernadotte (Michael Rennie), who was witness to the scene at Tallien's salon.

Years pass and, through his brilliant military campaigns and his wife Josephine's social influence, Napoleon rises in the government and eventually declares himself Emperor of France. At a court function Desiree again meets Bernadotte. Soon after, he proposes marriage to her and she accepts. Despite her marriage to Bernadotte, Napoleon continues to regard Desiree with affection and attempts to rekindle their romance on several occasions. She continually rebuffs him but an emotional connection remains for both.

Napoleon wages war on Europe and Bernadotte is one of the few who openly opposes his plans. Because of this the Swedish government approaches Bernadotte and offers him the position of heir to the throne of Sweden which he accepts. Bernadotte, Desiree, and their son Oscar renounce their French citizenship and move to Sweden. Desiree does

Napoleon meets Desiree's family (from left to right, Evelyn Varden, Richard Deacon, Marlon Brando, Jean Simmons, Cameron Mitchell, Elizabeth Sellars, and Isobel Elsom)

not fit in with the austere Swedish court and, after an argument with the Swedish queen, she goes back to Paris alone, promising to return to Bernadotte when his position in Sweden is more secure.

After his failed Russian campaign, Napoleon returns to France in defeat. He is briefly exiled but soon returns and makes an attempt to regain his former power. Fearing more violence and bloodshed, representatives of the French government approach Desiree. Knowing Napoleon's great fondness for her, they ask Desiree to intercede and convince him to surrender peacefully. Reluctantly, she goes to Chateau de Malmaison, where Napoleon has taken refuge, for one final confrontation with him.

The excellent background score for *Desiree* was composed by Alex North, however the main title music, "The Desiree Waltz", was written by Alfred Newman. This theme originally appeared in *Five Fingers* (1952) and would reappear as source music in *Justine* (1969). Ken Darby added

Desiree and Bernadotte (Michael Rennie)

lyrics to Newman's melody and it became the song "We Meet Again." This was recorded by Bing Crosby as the B side to his 1954 single "Who Gave You the Roses". Jane Froman also recorded it for her 1955 Capitol Records album "Jane Froman Sings".

13

Lord Vanity
by Samuel Shellabarger

> "When you say 'gentleman', my lady, there's a tone of mockery in your voice"
> – Richard Morandi

I FIRST HEARD ABOUT *Lord Vanity* in the documentary called *Hidden Hollywood: Treasures from the 20th Century-Fox Vaults*. The program was made up mostly of musical numbers that had been cut from Fox films. At the end of the show the hostess, Joan Collins, derisively says that she was also a victim of the cutting room floor. Actually in this case, a movie that never got made. The film was *Lord Vanity* and the footage shown in the documentary is a wardrobe and makeup test featuring Collins and Robert Wagner. Collins pokes fun at the clip ("I simply can't understand why THAT one didn't get made") but I was hooked and determined to find out more about this project that never saw the light of day.

From the title I assumed that *Lord Vanity* was a Beau Brummell type character, but I was wrong. After reading the novel I learned that the title is a metaphoric one. It refers to the main character Richard Morandi and his vain and selfish ways. Toward the end of the book there is a reflection on various things he had done in his life thus far: "Himself in every way currying favor here and there in the interests of his government, gaming, flattering, bribing, restless, his eye alert to the main chance. Certain it was that if God existed, He did not rule here nor in terms of the Black Mass offered to Lord Vanity…"

Once again we have a novel by Samuel Shellabarger. Published in 1953, this was his last work published before his death. The story, set in

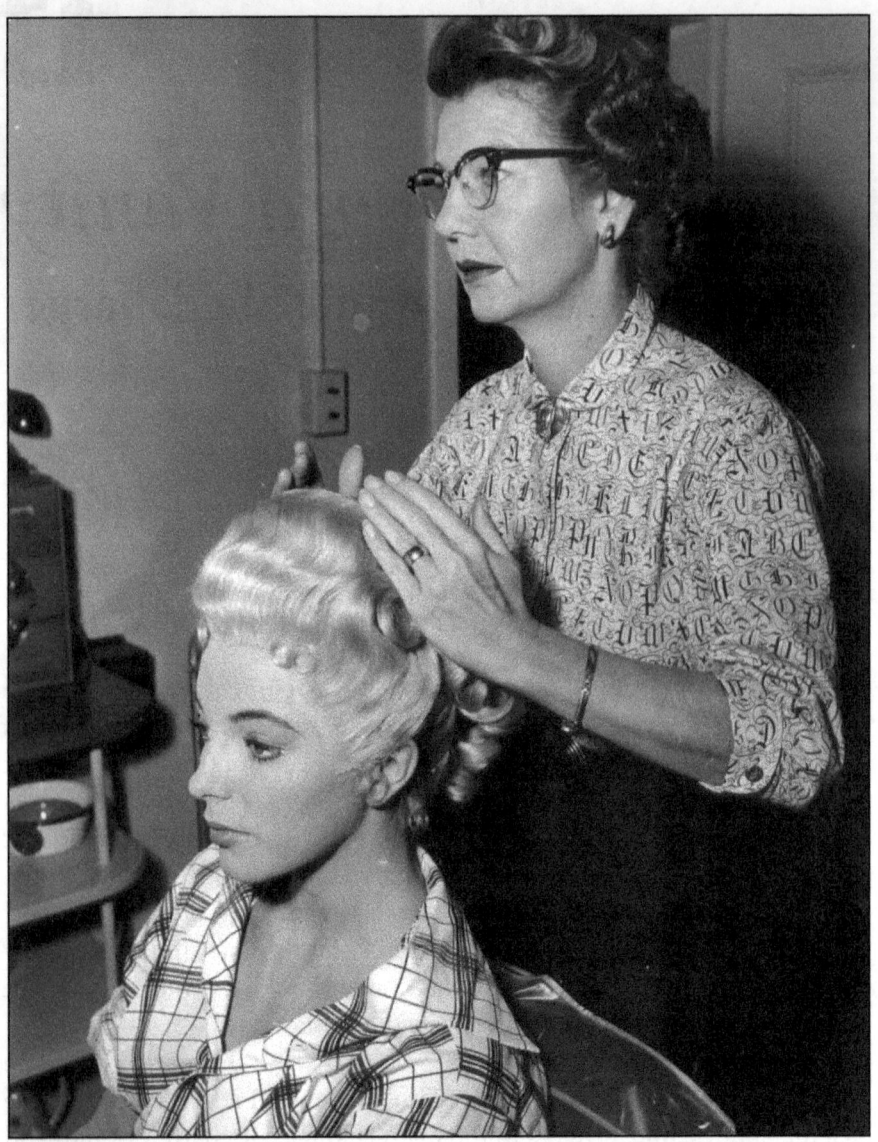

Joan Collins is readied for her screen test for Lord Vanity (Courtesy of Photofest)

the 18th century, revolves around Richard Morandi (later called Richard Hammond) who is the illegitimate son of an Englishman, Lord Marny, and a Venetian mother, Jeanne Morandi. Richard becomes involved with the conniving and unscrupulous Marcello Tromba who promises to help Richard attain the finer things in life…one way or another. Richard is torn between his lofty ambitions and his love for Maritza Venier, a ballet dancer

Lord Vanity • 223

who despises the type of life Richard is aspiring to achieve. The story takes Richard from Venice to France, England, the American Colonies, and Quebec. Much of the historical detail in the novel harkens back to one of Shellabarger's first books, a scholarly study called *Lord Chesterfield and His Works* published in 1935. *Lord Vanity* is a fascinating book and I think it would have made a wonderful movie. I do suspect, taking into consideration other Fox films of this type, the portions of the novel set in the New World would have been jettisoned to simplify the story.

THE MOVIE

The first information I could find on filming *Lord Vanity* appeared in Louella Parsons' column of June 6, 1953. Under the heading "ROBERT WAGNER LOOMS AS *LORD VANITY* STAR"

Parsons goes on to say that Darryl Zanuck bought the rights to the novel before any other company could bid on it and has already given the project to Charles Brackett, who would write the screenplay and produce the film. Robert Wagner is being considered to star. On December 4, 1953, Hedda Hopper's column says that producer Charles Brackett is ready to start *Lord Vanity* with Robert Wagner. Several months go by before the next mention of *Lord Vanity* in the gossip columns. On June 23, 1954 Sheila Graham rather belatedly confirms that Robert Wagner will indeed star in the CinemaScope production.

A preliminary outline for the *Lord Vanity* script, written by Charles Brackett and Walter Reisch, was submitted on June 19, 1953. By September 10, 1953 a Second Draft of the screenplay had been completed. A Final Draft screenplay dated July 15, 1954 was approved by Zanuck, although the script would be revised again in November 1954.

Meanwhile back in the gossip columns, October 1954 brought more news of *Lord Vanity*. Once again, Louella Parsons provides the scoop in her October 6 column headed, "CLIFTON WEBB WILL TURN VILLAIN". She says: "There's no character in comedy, drama, or melodrama that Clifton Webb can't play. Now he's been cast in the most villainous- and best- role he's had since *Laura* made him a top star. Clifton is set to play the adventurer [he was cast as Marcello Tromba] in *Lord Vanity*, Samuel Shellabarger's novel, a part which Shellabarger himself admitted was compounded of two Eighteenth Century figures- Lord Chesterfield and Cagliostro. Robert Wagner will play the title role, with Delmer Daves directing and Charles Brackett producing. The big hunt, Charlie says, is now on for another top star to portray Wagner's father, which also is a juicy part."

The next day national newspapers ran a United Press photo taken by Rene Henry with the following caption: "FACE LIFT FOR VERSAILLES PALACE, FRANCE....Workmen are busy doing a repair job on the stairs in the gardens of Versailles Palace, once used by French kings. The palace is getting a face-lift from 20th Century-Fox film company, which is slated to shoot the movie *Lord Vanity* in an authentic background."

In mid-October makeup and wardrobe tests were made of Robert Wagner, Clifton Webb, and Anna Maria Alberghetti (who would be playing Maritza Venier). Around this same time, Joan Collins was brought over from England to test for the part of Richard Morandi's lover Countess Amelie de Landres. For six weeks Collins did costume and makeup tests. The test footage, photographed by Milton Krasner, on view in *Hidden Hollywood*, was done on December 2, 1954. Shortly thereafter, Collins was rejected as being too young for the role and sent back to England.

Joan Collins and Robert Wagner in a test for *Lord Vanity*

In a 1955 *Modern Screen* interview Collins said she was "bruised by the experience" and "hated everything about Hollywood and everybody in it." Nevertheless, that same year Fox brought her back to Hollywood to appear in *The Virgin Queen* and put her under contract.

With Joan Collins out of the picture Darryl Zanuck decided that French actress Martine Carol would be perfect for the part but, in order to get her, the start date would have to be postponed until April 1955. At this point $600,000 had already been spent on the film. Director Delmer Daves later said, "[*Lord Vanity*] was a misguided thing right from the start. Zanuck had a pet second-unit director working abroad whom he wanted to keep on the payroll. So, he had this man, without any script because Charlie Brackett and Walter Reisch were still working on it, build a budget of way over $1 million of shooting location scenes in Italy, North Africa, Morocco. Darryl gave me the film to run and I didn't know what to do with it. This guy had lit canals in Venice for 18 blocks, and I asked Darryl what would happen to scenes like this if the story didn't call for them. He said 'Well, make it call for them.'" This all sounds like a lot of hogwash to me. If Daves was familiar with the script he would have known that the scenes of Venice were indeed "called for". The story opens with a festival in Venice. How North Africa and Morocco fit into this, I don't know. These are certainly not locations for *Lord Vanity*. Most likely the second unit was photographing locations for several pictures on this overseas junket.

On January 5, 1955, *Motion Picture Daily* announced that Martine Carol and Peter Ustinov had been added to the cast of *Lord Vanity*. Now the start date for the film had been pushed back to June. On April 21, 1955, Hollywood columnist Erskine Johnson reported, "Martine Carol feels about director husband Christian Jacques the way Ingrid Bergman feels about [Roberto] Rossellini. Won't do a movie unless he's at the helm. That's the reason why she's out of the cast of *Lord Vanity* and will make her first Hollywood movie with Jacques as the director." Apparently the departure of Martine Carol was a blow from which *Lord Vanity* never recovered. On July 27, 1955, Erskine Johnson wrote that *Lord Vanity* had been shelved, despite over a million dollars having been spent in preparation costs. Oddly the title was still listed as part of the forthcoming Fox lineup in the October 17, 1955 issue of *Daily Variety*.

In the 1988 book *Natalie and RJ: Hollywood's Star Crossed Lovers*, author Warren Harris offers another reason for the demise of *Lord Vanity*. After the departure of Martine Carol and while *Lord Vanity* was

Delmer Daves directs Joan Collins in her *Lord Vanity* screen test (Courtesy of Photofest)

in "casting limbo", Robert Wagner filmed the western *White Feather* in Durango, Mexico. He came down with severe amoebic dysentery and was unable to work for some time so *Lord Vanity* was put on hold. Harris states that by the time Wagner had recovered "Zanuck had resigned as studio head to become an independent producer for Fox based in Europe. His successor, Buddy Adler, had no enthusiasm for *Lord Vanity* or Robert Wagner, it seemed."

In his 2008 autobiography *Pieces of My Heart*, Robert Wagner mentions *Lord Vanity* briefly saying, "I was terribly excited by the opportunity to work with Errol Flynn." Flynn was cast as Wagner's father "Lord Marny" in the film. Wagner went to Warner Bros. to meet with Flynn but found him "in flagrante delicto" with a studio starlet. End of meeting. In 2016 playwright Mart Crowley asked his friend Robert Wagner about *Lord Vanity*. Wagner expressed his great disappointment that the film was never made. He recalled being coached in fencing and games of the period in which it took place. He said that Clifton Webb and Errol Flynn were in the cast and that the poor English of the leading lady

(Anna Maria Alberghetti) was a big problem. Wagner also said that Olivia de Havilland was set for a role (he couldn't recall which one) and that it was a "first class" production in every way.

A copy of the *Lord Vanity* script is included in the Hugh O'Brian Collection housed at UCLA. This would strongly suggest that he was also up for a role in the film but there is no notation on the script to verify in which part he might have been cast. Taking into consideration the villainous roles he had played prior to this in such films as *Back to God's Country* and *Son of Ali Baba* at Universal-International, O'Brian would have been perfectly cast as the conniving character "Sagredo". Shortly before his death, I contacted Hugh O'Brian's wife to see if he remembered anything about *Lord Vanity*, but he had no recollection of it at all.

What a pity that this interesting project with so much potential was "the one that got away."

Charlton Heston as Michelangelo in *The Agony and the Ecstasy*

14

The Agony and the Ecstasy
by Irving Stone

"It troubles me that princes and tyrants should have the right to order the lives of artists."

– Michelangelo

IRVING STONE (1903-1989) published his first book in 1934. It was a biographical novel about Vincent van Gogh called *Lust for Life* which was later made into a 1956 movie starring Kirk Douglas. Although he would also write non-fiction, the majority of Stone's output was in the biographical novel genre. He has often been credited with creating this type of book and he was the most successful of all the authors who wrote in this genre. In 1953 20th Century-Fox adapted his 1950 novel *The President's Lady* into a film starring Charlton Heston as Andrew Jackson and Susan Hayward as his beloved wife Rachel.

Irving Stone spent two years in Italy researching the life of Michelangelo in Florence and Rome. During this time he apprenticed with a sculptor so he could fully understand the workings of this art form. He had Michelangelo's letters translated into English and these served as the basis for the novel Stone wrote over the next four years. Stone said that he tried "to get inside the brain and heart of my subjects." *The Agony and the Ecstasy* was published by Doubleday in April 1961, was on the *New York Times* best seller list for 27 weeks, and sold twelve million copies the first year. In 1962 Stone published Michelangelo's letters in book form as *I Michelangelo, Sculptor*. Irving Stone's final book, *Depths of Glory*, is about the Impressionist painter Camille Pissarro and was published in 1985.

THE MOVIE

20th Century-Fox bought the rights to *The Agony and the Ecstasy* prior to publication and was already planning to make the film version in early 1962. By this time Darryl Zanuck had resigned as Chief of Production at Fox and the studio was being run into the ground by President Spyros Skouras. Philip Dunne, who had been away from Fox directing *The Inspector* in England, returned to the studio and his first assignment was to write and direct *The Agony and the Ecstasy*. Dunne wanted to turn it down because he felt "Stone's book was not drama but pure narrative: a popularized record of Michelangelo's entire life." Dunne's request was denied so he submitted a detailed treatment which he later admitted "used nothing of the book: it was an original invention based on the historical conflict between two strong-willed men, Michelangelo and Pope Julius II, which accompanied the painting of the Sistine Chapel's ceiling." To Dunne's surprise (and dismay) the studio loved his approach and he was given the go ahead to write the screenplay. He said, "I set Stone's massive tome aside, never to be opened again."

Dunne began to plan his screenplay with Spencer Tracy in mind for the Pope and Marlon Brando or Richard Burton for Michelangelo. He was even sent to Italy, to soak up some local color and present the idea to Richard Burton, who was then filming *Cleopatra* in Rome. Dunne observed first hand the production disaster that *Cleopatra* was quickly becoming. He returned to Los Angeles and had been working on the screenplay for two weeks when his agent called to tell him that his contract at Fox had been terminated. Dunne said, "And thus twenty-five years were at last wiped out by a twenty-five-second phone call." The runaway production costs of *Cleopatra* had used up any money there was to pay Fox employees and all work at the studio had been suspended.

Soon, Spyros Skouras was out and Darryl Zanuck was back in. One of the first projects that Zanuck threw out was *The Agony and the Ecstasy* but later, after reading Dunne's treatment, he decided to go ahead with it. At this point, Zanuck hoped to have Fred Zinnemann direct with Burt Lancaster as Michelangelo and Laurence Olivier as Pope Julius II.

Philip Dunne was rehired to complete the script which took him twelve weeks.

The $40 million eventual cost of *Cleopatra* almost ruined Fox and it would be another year before the studio could afford to produce a film on the scale that *The Agony and the Ecstasy* demanded. When it was finally ready to go into production, Charlton Heston had been cast

Philip Dunne

as Michelangelo and Rex Harrison as Pope Julius II. Fred Zinnemann turned down Fox's offer to direct, then Guy Green was considered but eventually Carol Reed was hired. Philip Dunne was unhappy that he had not been asked to direct but his admiration for Carol Reed helped him to overcome his disappointment.

After putting the finishing touches on the script, Philip Dunne travelled to Italy with Darryl Zanuck and Carol Reed to help pick the final locations and meet with Rex Harrison. In his autobiography Rex Harrison says he took the part, against his better judgement, mainly to work with his friend Carol Reed (plus a $250,000 pay check). It was not a happy experience for Harrison. Harrison said that Charlton Heston "very nicely made me feel that it was extremely kind of me to be supporting him." And he received no help from Carol Reed to assure him that his Pope was an equal role to Heston's Michelangelo. Heston, making lemonade out of lemons, said "[Rex] was quite temperamental, but that actually benefited the chemistry between the two of us in our on-screen relationship."

The movie was filmed in Italy from June 8 to September 7, 1964. Charlton Heston said, "In principal we had the Vatican's permission to shoot in the real Sistine Chapel, but when you thought about it, it was impossible. In the first place, the paintings were in terrible shape" (they would be restored in 1984). The studio would also have to shell out a huge amount of money for insurance coverage in case of damage. Consequently it was decided to recreate the Sistine Chapel at the Dino De Laurentiis Studios near Rome. Although the De Laurentiis sound stages were the largest in Europe at the time, they were not large enough to contain a full size recreation of the Sistine Chapel. Because of this, Production Designer John De Cuir had to create a set with interlocking mobile sections which could be assembled as needed. The reproduction of the fresco paintings was done utilizing 60 artists under the supervision of special art advisors Vincenzo LaBella and Professor Igino Cupelloni.

Once filming started, cinematographer Leon Shamroy took great pains in his lighting of the Sistine Chapel set and this slowed down the pace at which Carol Reed normally directed. Reed found this frustrating and he also objected to Robert D. Webb's handling of the second unit battle scenes. Rex Harrison felt that Reed wasn't himself throughout filming. Reed had just come off *Mutiny on the Bounty* where he had dealt with a very difficult Marlon Brando and was eventually replaced by Lewis Milestone as director. Harrison felt that because of this, Reed had become wary of actors and the power they had in the making of a picture.

Rex Harrison as Pope Julius II

Charlton Heston said, "Reed did not give either of us much guidance as to how he wanted us to perform."

With the exception of the Sistine Chapel sequences, interiors were shot at Cinecitta Studios. The location photography was done at Moneterano, the village of Todi, and in the marble quarries at Carrara. Regular players in Italian genre cinema, Fausto Tozzi, Alberto Lupo, Adolfo Celi, Rosalba Neri, Tomas Milian, and Daniele Vargas all have supporting roles but their voices are dubbed. The original budget had been estimated at $10 million but final costs were $7.2 million, which must have been a great relief for Zanuck, who was still trying to get the studio back on its financial feet.

Being their most expensive production of the year, Fox rightly decided to give *The Agony and the Ecstasy* a prestige roadshow release. In lieu of an overture, which usually begins these roadshow presentations, *The Agony and the Ecstasy* is preceded by a "Prologue" entitled "The Artist Who Did Not Want to Paint." This is a thirteen minute film, directed and written by Vincenzo LaBella, narrated by Marvin Miller, and scored by Jerry Goldsmith. It is a brief history of Michelangelo, focusing on his most famous sculptures, and serves as a perfect introduction to the film which follows.

In March 1965, Carol Reed and Charlton Heston attended a sneak preview of the finished film in Minneapolis where the audience gave it an enthusiastic reception. Thus, hopes were high when *The Agony and the Ecstasy* had its benefit premiere for the Metropolitan Museum of Art at the Lowe's State Theatre in New York City on October 7, 1965. Of course, Bosley Crowther at the *New York Times* didn't like it. He placed blame first on Philip Dunne's "wordy script" and second on Charlton Heston's

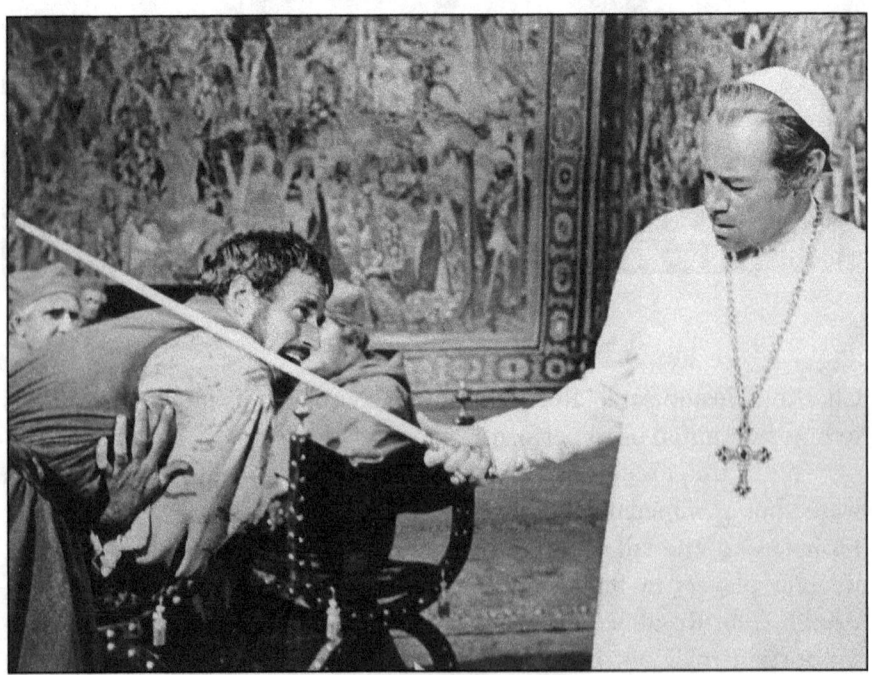

Rex Harrison must have played this particular scene with gusto

acting, which Boz found to be "arrogant, agonizing and cranky without a glimmer of ecstasy or warmth." Other critics were equally unkind. Dorothy Seiberling at *Life Magazine* thought the picture was filled with "phony situations, stereotyped characters, tawdry spectacles and two hours and twenty minutes of boredom." Judith Christ at *New York Herald Tribune* said it was "Dull, dull, dull, and unspectacular." One of the rare positive reviews came from *Variety* which found Philip Dunne's script to be "excellent" and the acting of both Rex Harrison and Charlton Heston "outstanding."

On October 20, the film had its West Coast premiere at the Carthay Circle Theatre in Los Angeles where it ran a successful 27 weeks. The *Los Angeles Herald Examiner* gave it a good review saying the film showed "a warm moving portrait of [Michelangelo's] personality."

The Agony and the Ecstasy opened in London at the Astoria Theatre on October 27. This was a Royal Premiere for the Duke of Edinburgh to benefit the Duke's Playing-Fields Charity. London reviews were also harsh. The terrible drubbing the picture took from the critics succeeded in keeping the patrons out of theaters for the most part and the film made a disappointing $8.2 million worldwide. The movie was nominated for five Academy Awards: Best Color Art Direction, Best Color Costume Design, Best Original Score, Best Sound Mixing, and Best Color Cinematography, winning none.

THE AGONY AND THE ECSTASY

Released: October 1965. Running time: 138 minutes.
In Todd-AO and Color by DeLuxe
Produced and Directed by Carol Reed
Screenplay by Philip Dunne
Music by Alex North.
Cinematography by Leon Shamroy
Edited by Samuel Beetley
Cast: Charlton Heston, Rex Harrison, Diane Cilento, Harry Andrews, Alberto Lupo, Adolfo Celi, Thomas Milian, Fausto Tozzi, Maxine Audley

In 1508, Pope Julius II (Rex Harrison) demands that Michelangelo (Charlton Heston) suspend the sculpture work he is doing on the Pope's tomb and instead begin working on painting frescos for the ceiling of the Sistine Chapel. Michelangelo, who considers himself to be more of a sculptor than a painter, resists the commission but the Pope forces him to accept. The work takes four years and throughout, the Pope and Michelangelo are at continual odds with each other. During this time the only people to provide emotional support and encouragement to Michelangelo are the Contessina de Medici (Diane Cilento) and her brother Giovanni (Adolfo Celi). Although their relationship is contentious, Pope Julius and Michelangelo both come to realize that their goal is the same; to produce a great and lasting work of art.

In his autobiography, *Take Two,* Philip Dunne says that the "downright hostile" reviews of *The Agony and the Ecstasy* puzzled him. Dunne felt "Perhaps the picture was not as good as I thought; I am certain it was not as bad as some of the critics thought." Both he and Darryl Zanuck considered it to be "as good an original script as I ever wrote" and that "Reed directed it superbly." Dunne did think that Zanuck had badly miscast the two leading roles; "With profound apologies to Chuck Heston and Rex Harrison, [I] would like to have seen my script played by Brando and Tracy or Burton and Tracy, *uomini terribili* all three, on and off the screen."

Charlton Heston was also taken aback by the poor reception given the film, "I was surprised and shocked by the negative response. I still consider my performance as Michelangelo as one of the finest of my career." Nicholas Warpshott's biography of Carol Reed relates that Heston claims he acquired Philip Dunne's script in October 1963 and convinced Fox to make the movie. As stated above, the project was in the works long before Heston was involved. More accurately, Charlton Heston was sent the script, liked the part, and signed his deal with Fox in October 1963. Heston also takes credit for "improving" the screenplay along with Carol Reed; "We cut a lot of literary crap out of the dialogue...writer's decoration that was just frosting on the scene." What an ego! Heston later said of his co-star, "I admire Rex enormously as an actor and feel he gave a remarkable performance as Pope Julius." Rex Harrison, on the other hand, remained bitter about Heston and continued to consider him a "very assuming fellow who thinks the world is his supporting cast." Years later when Heston and Harrison both appeared in the 1977 film *Crossed Swords*, they avoided any contact with each other on the set. Truth be told, both Heston and Harrison give terrific performances in *The Agony and the Ecstasy*, a truly remarkable and largely under appreciated motion picture, although its reputation has improved over the years.

The Artist and the Pope gaze at their great accomplishment

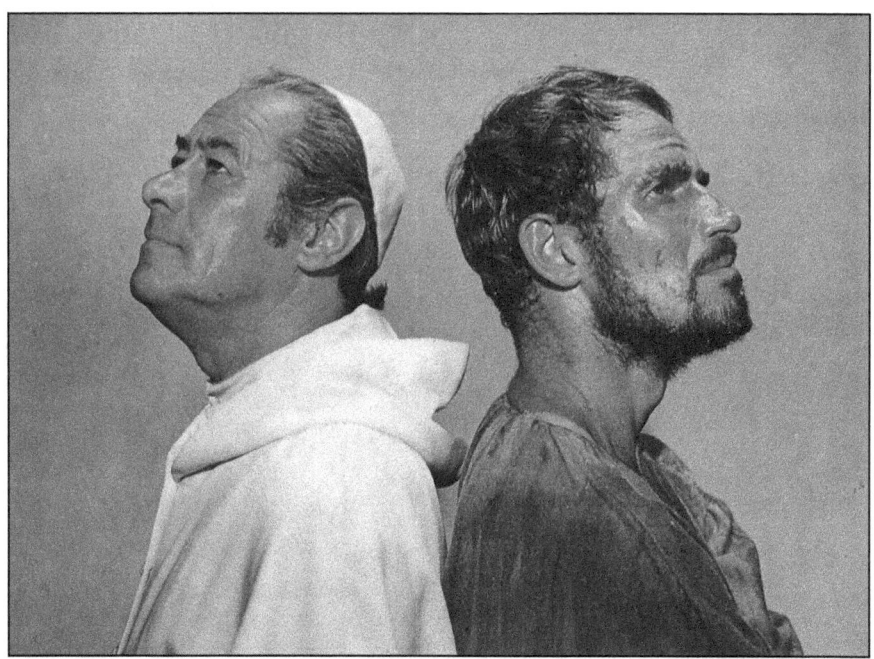

The photo says it all

The Agony and the Ecstasy is from a different time period than the other films in this book. I wanted to include a later Fox film but few of them were based on historical novels after the Fifties so the choices were limited. *Cleopatra* would have been a logical inclusion had the book that partially inspired it been more well known. The credits for *Cleopatra* claim it was "Based upon histories by: Plutarch, Suetonius, Appian, and other ancient sources and *The Life and Times of Cleopatra* by C.M. Franzero." Actually, much of the story structure and character development in the film version were drawn from Franzero's work. Carlo Maria Franzero's book had originally been published as a work of non-fiction in 1957. It was a straight forward historical account of Cleopatra, Julius Caesar, and Marc Antony. In 1962, while the film was still in production, Franzero's non-fiction book was adapted into a shorter historical novel called *Cleopatra* to be published as a paperback in conjunction with the film's 1963 release ("Read the Book...See the Movie!"). Whether or not Franzero did this adaptation is unclear. The British edition of the paperback has Franzero's original Preface while

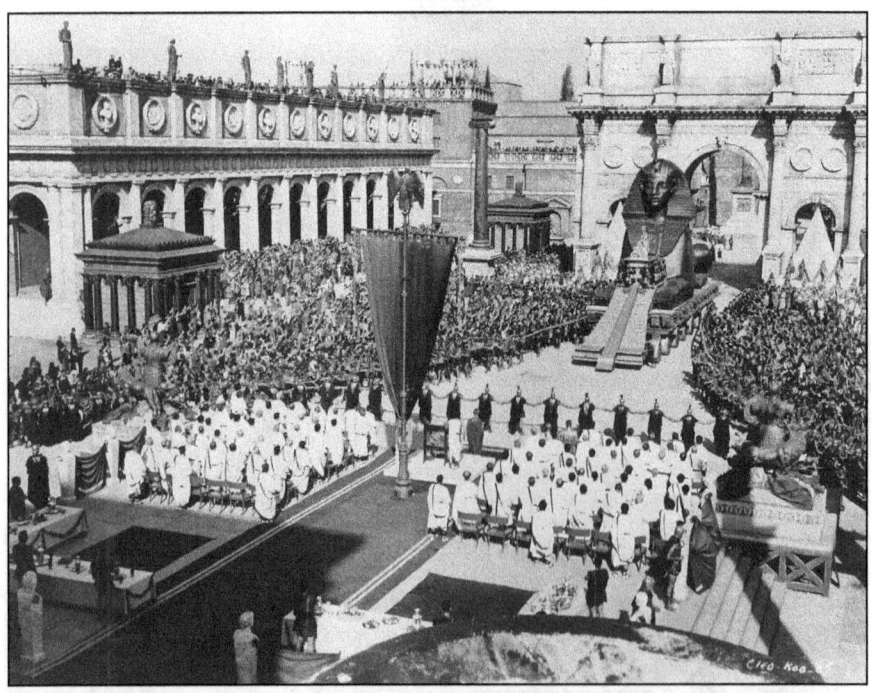

Cleopatra, the most spectacular 20th Century-Fox film of them all

the U.S. paperback does not. The novel version uses the framing device of a storyteller in a marketplace relating the history of Cleopatra to his audience. In 1968, *The Life and Times of Cleopatra* was re-published in its original form as part of a "Women Who Made History" series of books.

Afterword

"**The Times They Are a-Changin'**" says the Bob Dylan song… and that was written in 1964 so imagine how much "a-Changin" there has been since then. Many of the novels discussed in this book I hadn't read for decades. Re-reading them made me realize how much popular tastes have changed. For the most part, all of the books have a similar approach to the material at hand. Characterization is a strong point and there is usually a considerable amount of historical detail included. Vast amounts in some cases, proving that the authors certainly did an incredible amount of homework. A prime example is *Forever Amber* author Kathleen Winsor. Prior to writing her novel she claimed to have read over 350 books on the subject of King Charles II and the Restoration period. In the process, she amassed an impressive amount of information and made many detailed watercolor sketches. Yet when the novel came out, her exhaustive research was lost on reviewers who were too busy condemning the subject matter as "vulgar" or worse.

When Ms. Winsor died in 2003, many of her obituaries credited her for "launching the bodice ripper boom". The term "bodice ripper" is often said to have been coined by novelist Danielle Steel. The definition of "bodice ripper" in the Urban Dictionary says these books are "a sexually explicit romantic novel, usually in a historical setting." The entry goes on to say that the plots are "strictly formulaic" and "the genre is commercially highly successful but isn't taken seriously by most literary critics." The latter statement does rather sum up the reaction to *Forever Amber* but to dismiss the book in these terms is unjust. Few "bodice rippers" can boast the tremendous amount of historical research done by Ms. Winsor. The same can be said for Mika Waltari and *The Egyptian*. His interest in

Ancient Egypt was piqued when he did research for a play he wrote on the pharaoh Akhnaton. This eventually led to even more extensive research on 18th Dynasty Egypt when he decided to write *The Egyptian*. I was disheartened to learn that, despite its being highly acclaimed throughout most of the world, when *The Egyptian* was published in the United States in 1949 it was condemned as "obscene" in certain quarters.

Similarly, the merits of movie versions of these novels were often overlooked by the critics who tended to belittle them as mere popular entertainment. They were not deemed worthy of any serious consideration, no matter how much effort might have been put into the production. When I look at the nominees for the 1948 Academy Awards I am always stunned to see that the only recognition given to both *Captain from Castile* and *Forever Amber* is a single nomination each for Best Music Score (neither won). What happened to Art Direction, Costume Design, Color Cinematography? Surely both films should have been major contenders that year in all of these categories.

But I digress. I was discussing the novels. Reading these books takes a certain degree of concentration. There is a lot to take in. None of them is written in the now popular style which I call "toilet reading". The book that originally made me think of this description was Dan Brown's 2003 best seller *The Da Vinci Code*. The chapters were so brief that it seemed perfectly designed for toilet going (no comment on the content intended…maybe). As I look back on this, some of Stephen King's books precede this one in that respect, but the first time I noticed it was *The Da Vinci Code*. No one could ever accuse *The Egyptian* or *Prince of Foxes* of falling into this category.

Modern readers, like their moviegoing counterparts, might lack the patience for this type of storytelling. Everything now must be quick and to the point; no leisurely pacing allowed. Obviously what all this proves is that I am from another generation of book reading and film watching (aka "a dinosaur"). I like a book and movie that takes its time. Consequently I have a very soft spot for all of the books and movies I have included here. As many of the novels were written before I was born, in most cases I saw the film first (bless you NBC Saturday Night At the Movies!) and then read the book. This does reverse the publicity tag line I have used as the title of my little tome.

One last thought, several years ago a friend of mine wrote what I considered to be a brilliant historical novel about a knight in the Holy Land during the Crusades. The characters were finely drawn and the story was totally engrossing. He had spent years working on it and I saw his notebooks filled with information and sketches of swords, armor, goblets, and other Medieval paraphernalia pertaining to the time period of the story. As I read his draft I thought that if it had been written in the Forties, 20th Century-Fox would have snapped it up for Tyrone Power. He sent it to a publisher and they saw its merit but suggested that he remove most of the historical detail, which he had worked so hard to achieve, and beef up the sex. The publisher went on to say that nobody reads historical fiction anymore but they could probably sell it as a "romance novel" (aka "bodice ripper"). Discouraged and unwilling to compromise, my friend put his book away and forgot about it. He refused to accept that "The Times They Are a-Changin'."

Bibliography

Behlmer, Rudy. *Memo from Darryl F. Zanuck.* New York: Grove Press, 1993.

Belafonte, Dennis with Alvin H. Harill. *The Films of Tyrone Power.* Secacus, New Jersey: Citadel Press, 1979.

Brady, Frank. *Citizen Welles.* New York: Charles Scribner's Sons, 1989.

Bragg, Melvyn. *Richard Burton: A Life.* Boston: Little, Brown and Company, 1998.

Brynner, Rock. *Yul, the Man Who Would Be King.* New York: Simon & Schuster, 1989.

Cardiff, Jack. *Magic Hour: A Life in Movies.* London: Faber and Faber, 1996.

Davis, Ronald L. *Hollywood Beauty: Linda Darnell and the American Dream.* Oklahoma: University of Oklahoma Press, 1991.

Dunne, Philip. *Take Two.* New York: McGraw-Hill, 1980.

Eisner, Joel. *The Price of Fear: The Film Career of Vincent Price, In His Own Words.* Antelope Valley, California: Black Bed Sheet Books, 2013.

Eyman, Scott. *Ernst Lubitsch: Laughter in Paradise.* New York: Simon & Schuster, 1993.

Fujiwara, Chris. *The World and Its Double: The Life and Work of Otto Preminger.* New York: Faber and Faber, 2008.

Granger, Farley with Robert Calhoun. *Include Me Out*. New York: St. Martin's Press, 2007.

Guiles, Fred Lawrence. *Tyrone Power: The Last Idol*. New York: Doubleday & Company, 1979.

Gussow, Mel. *Darryl F. Zanuck: Don't Say Yes Until I Finish Talking*. New York: Da Capo Press, 1971.

Hanson, Patricia King (Executive Editor). *American Film Institute Catalog*. Berkeley: University of California Press, 1999.

Harris, Warren G. *Natalie and RJ: Hollywood's Star-Crossed Loves*. New York: Doubleday & Company, 1988.

Harrison, Rex. *Rex: An Autobiography*. New York: William Morrow & Company, 1974.

Hawkins, Jack. *Anything for a Quiet Life*. London: Elm Tree Books, 1973.

Heisner, Beverly. *Hollywood Art: Art Direction in the Days of the Great Studios*. Jefferson, North Carolina: McFarland & Company, 1990.

Heston, Charlton and Jean-Pierre Isbouts. *Charlton Heston's Hollywood*. New York: GT Publishing, 1998.

Higham, Charles. *Brando: An Unauthorized Biography*. New York: New American Library, 1987.

Krutnik, Frank with Steve Neale, Brian Neve, and Peter Stanfield. *"Un-American" Hollywood*. New Brunswick, New Jersey: Rutgers University Press, 2007.

Lipke, Alan Thomas. *The Strange Life and Stranger Afterlife of King Dick Including His Adventures in Haiti and Hollywood*. University of Florida, 2013.

Mosley, Roy with Philip and Martin Masheter. *Rex Harrison: A Biography*. New York: St. Martin's Press, 1987.

Moss, Robert F. *The Films of Carol Reed*. New York: Columbia University Press, 1987.

Munn, Michael. *Richard Burton: Prince of Players*. New York: Skyhorse Publishing, 2008.

O'Hara, Maureen with John Nicoletti. *'Tis Herself; A Memoir.* New York: Simon & Schuster, 2004.

Parla, Paul and Charles P. Mitchell. *Scream Sirens Scream!* Jefferson, North Carolina: McFarland & Company, 2009.

Pratley, Gerald. *The Cinema of Otto Preminger.* New York: A.S. Barnes & Company, 1971.

Robinson, Jay with Jim Hardiman. *The Comeback.* Lincoln, Virginia: Chosen Books, 1979.

Smith, Steven C. *A Heart at Fire's Center: The Life and Music of Bernard Herrmann.* Berkeley, California: University of California Press, 1991.

Solomon, Aubrey. *20th Century-Fox: A Corporate and Financial History.* Latham, Maryland: Scarecrow Press, 2002.

Staggs, Sam. *Inventing Elsa Maxwell.* New York: St. Martin's Press, 2012.

Thomas, Tony and Aubrey Solomon. *The Films of 20th Century-Fox.* Secaucus, New Jersey: Citadel Press, 1979.

Thompson, Frank with David Shepard and Ted Perry. *Henry King: Director.* Los Angeles, California: Directors Guild of America Publishing, 1995.

Tierney, Gene with Mickey Herskowitz. *Self Portrait.* Wyden Books, 1978.

Wagner, Laura. *Anne Francis: The Life and Career.* Jefferson, North Carolina: McFarland & Company, 2011.

Wagner, Robert J. with Scott Eyman. *Pieces of My Heart.* New York; Harper Collins Publishers, 2008.

Wapshott, Nicholas. *Carol Reed: A Biography.* New York: Alfred A. Knopf, 1994.

Weaver, Tom. *Double Feature Creature Attack.* Jefferson, North Carolina: McFarland & Company, 2003.

Williams, Lucy Chase. *The Complete Films of Vincent Price.* New York: Citadel Publishing, 1995.

Index

Addams, Dawn 157-158
Agony and the Ecstasy, The 228-238
Alberghetti, Anna Maria 224, 227
Aldon, Mari 56, 64
Allgood, Sara 56, 64
Anna and the King 49
Anna and the King of Siam 7, 36-49, 70, 114
Annabella 13, 90, 104
Antoine, Le Roi 132, 139
Arthur, Jean 29
Aubrey, Cecile 112, 118-119, 121, 123-124

Ball, Jane 29
Bancroft, Anne 22, 174
Beard, Rene 77
Benjamin Blake 8-23
Benson, Sally 38
Bergman, Ingrid 150, 225
Berti, Marina 102, 110
Big Fisherman, The 148, 169, 179-180
Black Rose, The 112-127
Blaustein, Julian 211-213
Bogarde, Dirk 191
Boone, Richard 167
Boyer, Charles 38
Brackett, Charles 45-46, 223, 225
Brando, Marlon 183, 185, 190-191, 193, 208, 212-214, 216-219, 230, 232
Brazzi, Rossano 131
Bride of Vengeance 106
Brown, Vanessa 72, 78, 150
Brynner, Yul 45-49

Buckmaster, John 157-159
Burton, Richard 146, 153-154, 157-158, 164, 166, 168, 230

Cady, Jerome 5, 53, 70
Captain from Castile ix, 6, 78, 81-97, 100, 117
Cardiff, Jack 120
Carol, Martine 225
Caron, Leslie 118
Cassavetes, John 191
Chandler, Jeff 10, 25, 153
Chretien, Henri 153
Christian, Linda 91, 104, 118, 200, 206
Cleopatra 230-231, 238-239
Clift, Montgomery 193, 212
Cluny Brown 31, 55
Cobb, Lee J. 94-95
Collins, Joan 221-222, 224-226
Cooper, Gladys 157
Costain, Thomas B. 113, 117, 121
Coward, Noel 212
Cregar, Laird 13, 27
Cromwell, John 12, 38, 40, 70
Cummins, Peggy 38, 54-56, 61, 64, 116, 118
Currie, Finlay 22, 23, 122
Curtiz, Michael 183, 188-190, 193-194, 196

Dandridge, Dorothy 47, 72
Dark Angel, The 183
Darnell, Linda 42-43, 50, 56, 59-62, 64, 66, 72, 84-86, 117, 130-131, 135

Darvi, Bella 182, 185, 188-190, 200, 203, 206-207
Daves, Delmer 20, 158, 169, 172, 223, 225-226
Davis Bette 179, 183
De Havilland, Olivia 38, 227
Demetrius and the Gladiators 142, 169-178, 212
DeMille, Cecil B. 101, 192, 197
Desiree ix, 78, 187, 191, 208-220
Domergue, Faith 185
Douglas, Kirk 185-186, 188, 190-191, 207
Douglas, Lloyd C. 2, 147, 151, 169, 179-180
Dragonwyck 24-35
Dunne, Irene 36, 38, 40, 42-43
Dunne, Philip 11-12, 53, 56-58, 136-137, 151-152, 164, 170, 184, 188, 190, 193, 196, 230-232, 234, 236

Egan, Richard 174-176
Egyptian, The 6, 181-207, 212, 242
Eythe, William 29

Farmer, Francis 13-14, 16
Fleming, Victor 151
Flynn, Errol 54, 133, 226
Forever Amber 6, 39, 50-67, 70, 72, 86, 93, 100, 115-117
Foxes of Harrow, The 68-80
Francis, Anne 133, 135-137, 139-141, 144-145

Gardner, Ava 185
Gilmore, Virginia 12, 46
Goddard, Paulette 86, 106-107
Gone With the Wind 1-3, 5-6, 51-52, 74, 163, 210
Goulding, Edmund 54
Grahame, Margot 57-59, 62, 64
Granger, Farley 191
Green Dolphin Street 91
Greene, Richard 54, 57, 72
Gwenn, Edmund 13

Hanover Square 27
Harrison, Rex 38-43, 68, 70-72, 74-77, 79-80, 232-237
Hathaway, Henry 114, 117, 121
Hawkins, Jack 118-121, 123-125
Haydn, Richard 56-57, 60, 78
Hayward, Susan 7, 54, 131-132, 170, 173-175, 178, 229
Hendrix, Wanda 101, 104-105, 107-109
Hepburn, Audrey 213
Herrmann, Bernard 42, 195, 207
Heston, Charlton 228-229, 231-237
How to Marry a Millionaire 162
Hughes, Howard 151

Inda, Estela 95-96

Jennings, Talbot 38, 114, 122
Johnson, Kay 12, 20
Jones, Jennifer 5, 86, 150

Katherine 6, 26
Kaus, Gina 151
Kaye, Danny 103
Kazan, Elia 38
Kerr, Deborah 47-49
King and I, The 6, 7, 44-48
King Dick 129-130, 135, 137, 140-142
King, Henry 4, 85-86, 88-89, 100, 102-105, 120
Korngold, Erich Wolfgang 150
Koster, Henry 152, 156, 158, 162, 164, 212-214

Lamarr, Hedy 132, 135
Lancaster, Burt 153, 185
Lanchester, Elsa 17-18
Landis, Carole 79-80
Landon, Margaret 37, 44, 48
Lang, Walter 46-48
Langan, Glenn 29, 33-34, 56-57, 60
Lardner, Ring Jr. 57-58
Lawrence, Barbara 91-92
Lawrence, Gertrude 44-45
Lee, Rowland V. 179-180

Leigh, Vivien 2, 3, 54, 193, 211
LeRoy, Mervyn 150
Lighton, Louis D. 38, 40, 114, 117
Litvak, Anatole 211
Lloyds of London 3- 4
Longest Day, The 163
Lord Vanity 6, 81, 83, 221-227
Lubitsch, Ernst 26, 31, 38
Lupino, Ida 13
Lydia Bailey 128-145

Madame Phang 125, 127
Maltz, Albert 150-152
Mankiewicz, Joseph L. 26-27. 29-31, 83
Marshall, Edison 9-10, 19
Marshall, William 128, 132-133, 135, 137-143, 177
Mason, James 70, 153
Mature, Victor 101, 153, 155, 157, 164-166, 169-172, 174, 176-177, 185-186, 188, 190, 195-198, 204-205, 212
McKracken, Booth 105
McDowall, Roddy 11, 15
Medina, Patricia 72-73, 77
Mitchell, Cameron 188, 214, 218-219
Mitchell, Margaret 1, 51
Monroe, Marilyn 162, 185
Moreno, Rita 47, 216
Morgan, Henry 30
Morrow, Jeff 159-161
Murphy, Audie 101, 104

Negulesco, Jean 135, 162
Nesbitt, Cathleen 215-216
Newman, Alfred 14, 92, 165, 195, 219
North, Alex 219
Northwest Passage 137

Oberon, Merle 213-214, 217-218
Olivier, Laurence 153, 193, 211
O'Brian, Hugh 188, 227
O'Hara, Maureen 13, 147, 54, 70-72, 75-78

Paget, Deborah 171, 174-175, 185
Papich, Stephen 160, 163
Peck, Gregory 27, 70, 118, 150-151
Perlberg, William 11, 53
Peters, Jean 82, 89-90, 93-96, 153, 184
Powell, William 38
Power, Tyrone 4-5. 8, 11, 13, 16-19, 82-83, 85-88, 90-98, 100-105, 107-110, 112, 118-120, 122-125, 127, 132-133, 135, 143, 153, 185, 206
Preminger, Otto 21, 26, 31, 47, 56, 58, 125
President's Lady, The 229
Price, Vincent 5, 24, 27-35, 55, 88-89
Prince of Foxes 83, 98-111, 120
Purdom, Edmund 182, 191-193, 197-198, 200-204, 206, 213

Racers, The 207, 211
Reed, Carol 232-234, 236
Reisch, Walter 223, 225
Revere, Anne 33-34, 57, 64
Robe, The 6-7, 146-180, 183, 187, 203
Roberts, Kenneth 129-130, 135, 137
Robertson, Dale 134-135, 138-141, 144
Robinson, Casey 183-184
Robinson, Jay 158, 160, 166, 168, 171-174, 176-178, 186-187, 212
Rodgers and Hammerstein 45, 47
Romero, Cesar 87-88, 93, 96
Ross, Frank 148-152, 158, 162, 174
Rotunno, Giuseppe 100
Russell, John 57, 59-61, 64

Sanders, George 13, 15, 57, 60, 67
Selinko, Annemarie 209-211, 215, 217
Selznick, David O. 2-3, 38, 52, 86
Seton, Anya 6, 25
Shamroy, Leon 48, 60, 100, 105, 166, 200, 232
Shellabarger, Samuel 6. 81, 98, 221-223
Shock 28-29
Simmons, Jean 153-154, 156-158, 162, 166, 168, 185, 190, 200, 208, 211, 213-215, 217-220

Skouras, Spyros 59, 230
Snows of Kilimanjaro, The 183-184
Son of Fury 10, 12-19, 21, 23
Sondergaard, Gale 42, 44
Stahl, John M. 38, 54, 56, 70-72
Stevens, Anitra 187-188
Stone, Irving 229-230
Stuart, Randy 76
Sutton, John 88-89, 93

Tandy, Jessica 29, 56, 61, 67
Taradash, Daniel 210
Ten Commandments, The 46, 192, 197
Tierney, Gene 8, 13-14, 16, 24, 26, 31-35, 54, 56, 184, 190, 194-195, 205
Tracy, Spencer 137, 152, 230
Treasure of the Golden Condor 10, 19-23
Trotti, Lamar 85-86
Turner, Lana 56, 91

Ustinov, Peter 190, 194, 198, 225

Virgin Queen, The 179, 225

Wagner, Robert 179, 221, 223-224, 226
Waltari, Mika 181-184, 241
Ward, Billy 72. 74, 77
Waxman, Franz 165, 174, 195
Webb, Clifton, 103, 121, 144-145, 223-224, 226
Webb, Robert D. 90, 121, 223
Welles, Orson 102-103, 105-107, 110-111, 120-121, 123
Wheeler, Lyle 40, 41, 196
White, Walter 133, 137-138
Whitney, Peter 55, 64
Wilde, Cornel 20-23, 54, 56-58, 60, 72, 83-84, 115, 117-118
Wilding, Michael 187, 194-195, 202, 204, 213
Williams, Annie Laurie 2, 51
Winsor, Kathleen 51-53, 241
Wray, Fay 20
Wynter, Dana 188

Yerby, Frank 69, 75

Zanuck, Darryl F. Nearly every page in the book

www.ingramcontent.com/pod-product-compliance
Lightning Source LLC
Chambersburg PA
CBHW071705160426
43195CB00012B/1580